Penguin Books

The Markets of London

Born and educated in Cambridge, Alec Forshaw
has spent the last sixteen years in London, where
he works as Conservation Officer in Islington and
spends his spare time playing music, writing and,
most recently, visiting all of London's markets on
his bicycle. His fascination for the history and
character of London life has led to a number of
books on the subject, including *Smithfield Past and
Present*, *The Open Spaces of London* and *The Square
Mile*.

Theo Bergström was born in Leicester and for the
last twenty years has been a highly successful professional photographer in London, producing illustrated books and advertising material and holding
exhibitions of his work. His previous publications
include *Stonehenge*, *Hadrian's Wall*, *The Thames*, *Beer
Naturally*, *Light Fantastic*, *Smithfield Past and Present*
and *The Open Spaces of London*.

Alec Forshaw and Theo Bergström

Penguin Books

Maps reproduced by permission of Geographers' A–Z Map Co.
Ltd and with the permission of the Controller of Her Majesty's
Stationery Office, Crown Copyright reserved.

PENGUIN BOOKS

Published by the Penguin Group
27 Wrights Lane, London W8 5TZ, England
Viking Penguin Inc., 40 West 23rd Street, New York, New York 10010, USA
Penguin Books Australia Ltd, Ringwood, Victoria, Australia
Penguin Books Canada Ltd, 2801 John Street, Markham, Ontario, Canada L3R 1B4
Penguin Books (NZ) Ltd, 182–190 Wairau Road, Auckland 10, New Zealand

Penguin Books Ltd, Registered Offices: Harmondsworth, Middlesex, England

First published 1983
Reprinted with revisions 1986
Reprinted with further revisions 1989

Photographs copyright © Theo Bergström, 1983, 1986, 1989
Text copyright © Alec Forshaw, 1983, 1986, 1989
All rights reserved

Made and printed in Great Britain by
Butler & Tanner Ltd, Frome and London
Filmset in Baskerville

Designed by Jessica Smith

The picture on the title page shows an aerial view of
Petticoat Lane market

Contents

Introduction

London is a market town. It started as a trading post, built by the Romans at the lowest point where they could cross the River Thames. Its position as a sea port and river crossing has enabled London to grow into one of the world's great cities. Markets are and always will be its lifeblood, through the exchange and dealing in commodities from all corners of the globe, the associated businesses of insurance, shipping and banking, and the physical distribution of goods, wholesale and retail, throughout London.

No other city can match the number and variety of London's markets, ranging from the shabby daily street markets selling cabbages and cucumbers to the rarefied floor of the Stock Exchange. Which other city can rival the magnificence or history of London's great wholesale markets? The sprawling urban mass we call London is a collection of many towns and villages, posh and poor. Each has its own marketplace which betrays the local character, heart on sleeve.

Markets provide vitality, fun and good value. For those who never venture beyond the respectable suburbs or the West End, the markets of east London are a social education; here people work to live and the market faces are an eccentric amalgam of grotesque gargoyles, bovine placidity and friendly humour. When so much has been swept away by bombs and planners, markets, like pubs, continue old traditions and keep communities together, defying the new Brutalism. Despite the emergence of supermarkets and multiple chain stores, Londoners still love to shop in markets, and while some of the famous nineteenth-century street markets have dwindled or been extinguished by redevelopment, new markets have sprung up to replace them, such as Swiss Cottage, Camden Passage and Jubilee Market. Others have been boosted by Asian, Caribbean and Middle Eastern immigrants for whom the street market is the nearest thing to their native bazaars. Many markets, like fairs, attract the transient and feckless – street performers, tricksters and pickpockets who thrive amongst the chaos of jostling crowds.

The soul of London's markets, the tens of thousands of porters and stallholders are hardened to the long hours and weathered by the wind and rain. For generations they have pulled their market barrows, living among the smell of cabbage ends, gutters and fish oil. The flower lady who has spent fifty years sitting on a rickety chair beside her stall selling daffs and chrysanths has seen it all, and yet still calls you 'darling' for your pains. In the backstreets of Walworth and Shoreditch craftsmen build and repair the traditional wooden barrows, gaily painted, elegantly carved and with sturdy metal-rimmed wheels. These are the characters who keep the markets alive.

This book traces the origins and growth of markets in London throughout its long history and describes individually the existing retail and wholesale markets of inner London. Not all retail markets are easily categorized as 'general' or 'specialist'. The reader may disagree with the classification of Portobello Road or Petticoat Lane markets, known for their specialism but also, owing to their size, offering a good variety.

For those using the book as a guide, a word of warning: opening times are as observed by the author, not necessarily the official or licensed hours. Bus-route information is correct for Summer 1988.

Through lack of space I have omitted a detailed survey of the suburbs, and I have also left out many of the indoor shopping arcades which call themselves markets, such as Antiquarius, Gray's Antique Market or Kensington Market. Even without these the spectrum is wide, the diversity astonishing. To find out what London is like, go to its markets.

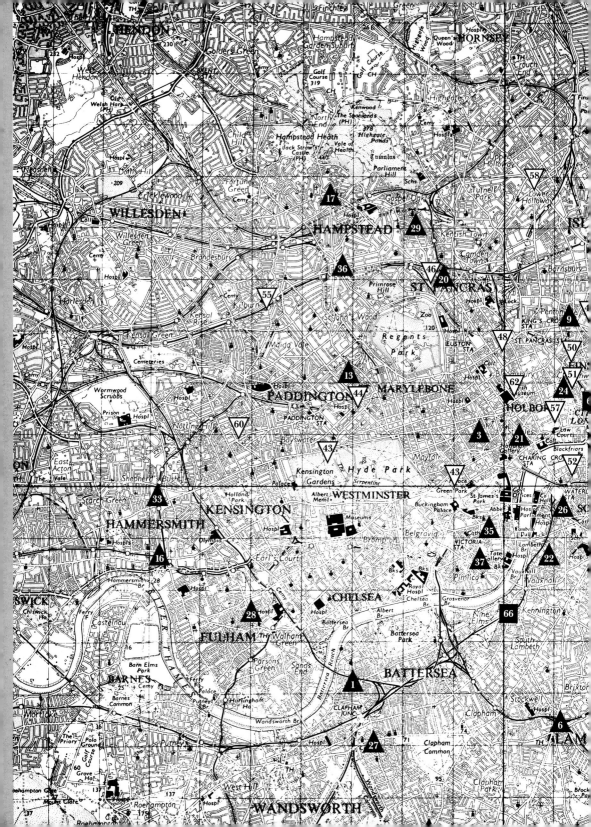

The Markets of London

Map showing the location of the markets in London

▲ General Retail Markets

▽ Specialist Retail Markets

■ Wholesale Markets

(For key to the numbers refer to the bracketed numbers on the Contents page)

The Development of London's Markets

Medieval Beginnings

The recent discovery of the northern bridgehead of the original Roman London Bridge near the Monument provided the final proof of the early importance of London as a trading centre and market town. Roman Londinium, founded in about 43 A.D., was more than a military garrison on the north bank of the River Thames; the bridge across the Thames established a vital link between the agriculturally productive south-east and the hostile lands to the north. After their military conquest the Romans were quick to incorporate their new province into the economic structure of the empire. Britain became a supplier and consumer of goods from all parts of the Roman dominion: pottery, wine, bronze, glass, olive oil, lead, pewter, corn, wool and salt. The Thames estuary was an easily navigable route to the open seas and ports of Europe, and Londinium developed rapidly as the Romans' main distribution centre for British and foreign produce.

At the centre of the walled Londinium the Romans built a marketplace or forum, a large square 200 yards across, which occupied a site approximately where Gracechurch Street and Leadenhall are now. Wholesalers and retailers thrived next to the basilica, town hall and courts of justice, and so it continued for nearly four hundred years – chief port and financial centre of Britain.

After 410 A.D. London was overrun by Saxon raiders and abandoned to the ravages and mysteries of the Dark Ages. By the seventh century it was re-established as a trading centre: merchants dealing in leather, cloth, timber and grain were flourishing, and the Thames resumed its role as London's backbone and lifeline. The tidal river had eroded the old Roman waterfront and new timber and stone wharves were built along the north bank. Water-borne trade was concentrated at the jetties of Billingsgate and Queenshythe, handling imports of fish, salt, wool, coal and wood.

Inside the town two open retail markets evolved in late Saxon times: Westcheap and Eastcheap. 'Ceap' was the Anglo-Saxon word for market, and as a verb meant 'to barter'. Westcheap, known later as Cheapside, formed an east–west axis from

Newgate to where the Bank is today. Eastcheap was nearer the river, where Cannon Street and East Cheap are now. Westcheap was the larger market and occupied the City's widest street. On holy days the Normans held processions and jousts there and introduced regulations controlling the market. The open stalls were ordered to stand midway between the kennels or gutters, allowing carts and pedestrians to pass either side.

Westcheap was the main food market, selling largely local produce. Within the City walls gardens and allotments were crammed with vegetables and herbs – leeks, onions, cabbages, garlic and parsley. Outside the walls the farmland within a thirty-mile radius supplied the rest of London's food – wheat for bread, cattle for beef, milk, cheese and eggs. Many London households kept pigs and poultry while swans and ducks were abundant on the river. From dawn to dusk on market day Cheapside was crowded with country folk, their merchandise laid out on tables or in baskets in the middle of the road. A bell sounded the end of trading an hour or so before the curfew bell sent respectable citizens scuttling home to their beds.

London grew steadily within the old Roman walls, despite the setbacks of the Black Death and other outbreaks of plague. Cheapside market expanded into side streets and even into St Paul's churchyard. Some intrepid stallholders and letter-writers sought the cover of the cathedral nave until marketing in the church was condemned and banned by Bishop Braybrook in 1385. One wonders how he would react to the tourist souvenir stalls in the cathedral today! Different sections of Cheapside specialized in particular produce, and names of side streets remain to indicate the different commodities – Bread Street, Wood Street, Ironmonger Lane, Honey Lane, Milk Street and, at the eastern end, Poultry. Unlike today honey was the main source of sweetening, sugar being a rare luxury, only for the rich. Heating and cooking depended on firewood and huge bundles were carried in from the woods and forests near London such as St John's Wood, Soho and Hampstead. Bread Street was renowned for its concentration of bakers by 1100; a royal

(*overleaf*) Little Earl Street, Covent Garden 1913 (G.L.C.)

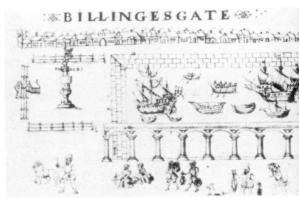

Medieval Eastcheap sold mainly meat and offal; Billingsgate, corn, coal and wool as well as fish (Guildhall Library)

decree in 1300 forbade bread to be sold anywhere else, even bread baked outside London and brought in by cart, so that weights and prices could be controlled.

Trades and professions grouped together to protect their own interests. Stallkeepers were constantly subjected to trading regulations and pressure from traffic, so merchants banded together into associations or guilds which, over the centuries, acquired political and financial power. The greatest wealth derived from imports. The north bank of the river was lined with public and private wharves, their names denoting the cargoes – Garlickhythe, Hays Wharf, Wool Quay. Medieval Londoners consumed vast quantities of garlic. Fresh meat was in short supply, often rancid or tough, salted in winter, and requiring strong seasoning to render it palatable. Curry houses have re-awakened our medieval taste buds!

The mercers were the wealthiest and most influential company. Between 1200 and 1334, out of 250 City Aldermen a quarter were wool merchants, a quarter cloth merchants and a quarter wine merchants. In 1290 the Jews who had colonized Old Jewry were expelled from Britain, not to return for five centuries. The Lombards from Italy took over the vacant financial role. Certain foreign merchants were granted special privileges and freedoms, like the Hanseatic League from north

Germany who rented a yard in Thames Street. Craftsmen of common trades clustered in separate quarters, the grocers in Bucklersbury, goldsmiths in Foster Lane, grain merchants in Cornhill, poulterers in Poultry, mercers in Cheapside, skinners in Budge Row (lamb's skin was called 'boge'). The wealthier guilds or companies built their own livery halls.

At the time of the Norman Conquest Eastcheap was the main meat market, selling beef, pies and offal. Offal was called 'puddings' and butchers were allowed to use Pudding Lane for access to the river to dump their entrails. Eastcheap was hampered by its narrowness, and it declined as new markets sprang up elsewhere in the medieval City to complement the great market at Cheapside. Butchers congregated increasingly in the Shambles market at Newgate, conveniently close to the livestock market which had become established at Smithfield just outside the City wall. The Stocks market started in 1280 on a site later to be occupied by Mansion House, selling fish, poultry and a wide variety of game. Londoners had catholic tastes – swans, geese, pheasants, curlews, thrushes and blackbirds (hence 'four and twenty blackbirds, baked in a pie'). The market was named after the nearby pillory where miscreants were punished – nothing to do with the Stock Exchange! The market was enlarged in 1410 after which it sold fruit and vegetables in place of meat and fish. The meat trade moved to Leadenhall which became a market when the old lead-roofed manor was demolished. Leadenhall market was reserved specifically for country poulterers who were not allowed to trade in Cheapside, and stalls soon spread into the adjacent Lime Street and Gracechurch Street.

Bear Quay, Queenshythe and Cornhill specialized in grain and hay; corn was threshed and winnowed, separating the bran and chaff, in Seething Lane. Smithfield cattle and hay market was well established by 1100; so was the fruit and vegetable market on London Bridge which moved to Borough High Street in 1276, the predecessor of Borough market.

Fish was a major part of the diet. Religious observance ruled out meat for up to 150 days per year. In any event meat was expensive and often of poor quality; oysters from the Thames were food for the poor. Fishmongers huddled in Fish Street Hill near the landing stages of Billingsgate, but the daily market was augmented on the busiest day of the week by Friday Street. William Walworth, Lord Mayor and subjugator of Wat Tyler, was a fishmonger; as a guild the fishmongers were disliked for their monopolistic power and price control. They encouraged legislation enforcing 'fish days' and fostered the fear that a decline in fish consumption would reduce the numbers of fishermen/sailors for the King's navy and cause coastal towns to decay.

Market customs and practices were carefully governed by laws and proclamations, many of which are still relevant today. The right or franchise to hold a market (that is, a concourse of buyers and sellers disposing of commodities) was granted by royal privilege, usually in the form of a charter from the Crown. From Saxon times market rights were vigorously protected and unauthorized trading outside the marketplace and market hours prevented. Different kinds of food had by law to be sold in specified market areas at specified times, notified

London Bridge in 1616, with Southwark Cathedral in the foreground and traitors' heads on the gate. The vegetable market moved from the bridge to Borough High Street in 1276 (Museum of London)

by the ringing of a bell, so that quality could be inspected.

'Every man who brings Thames fish for sale, taken to the east of London Bridge, shall stand in Cornhill to sell the fish, and nowhere else, on pain of forfeiture of the fish' (City Regulations, 1388). Established stallholders within authorized markets during daylight hours enjoyed the privileges and immunities of 'market overt'. Goods, so long as they were not defective, could not be queried. The present-day problem of tracing stolen goods through a market derives from market overt. Only a few products, such as dried fish, were allowed to be sold door-to-door by hawkers or 'birlesters'.

Consumer protection was accompanied by fierce punishment for offenders: bakers were fined or flogged for selling substandard loaves, while a butcher caught with rancid meat or a fishmonger with putrid fish might have it burnt under his nose sitting in the pillory at the Stocks market.

Bartholomew Fair, depicted in the eighteenth century, but with strong medieval traditions (Museum of London)

Fairs were as important as regular markets for the exchange of goods. By the 1200s a network of fairs was established throughout Europe which included the great annual fairs of St Denis in northern France, and Stourbridge near Cambridge. Although the French wars caused a shift from France to the Flemish markets of Bruges, Antwerp and Ghent, London continued to be a crucial cog in European trade, importing wine, pottery and metals and exporting coal, corn, cloth and wool. The thirteenth- and fourteenth-century English economy was based on wool – there were three sheep for every person in England – and wool exports attracted special customs duty. Most of it passed through the great cloth fair held every August beside the Priory of St Bartholomew in Smithfield. The merchant taylors and mercers ensured fair trading at Bartholomew Fair using special piepowder courts to administer instant and summary justice to vagabonds and vagrants. Piepowder derives from *pieds poudrés*, literally dusty feet, as disputants had no time to dust themselves down before appearing. Harrow Pie House in High Capers, just off West Street, is the surviving court house from the annual fair at Harrow-on-the-Hill, founded in 1262 and abolished in 1850.

Fairs were usually held on religious or pagan holidays such as Easter, May Day, Midsummer, Michaelmas and Christmas. At Bartholomew Fair and Southwark Fair on the south side of London Bridge mystery plays, pageants, bear- and bull-baiting and sideshows accompanied and later overshadowed the serious business of trading.

In the twelfth century London's population was about 40,000, the equivalent of a small country market town, and probably less than the population of Londinium in its heyday. The Black Death and less spectacular outbreaks of plague continually limited population growth. Even by 1500 there were no more than 75,000 inhabitants, and large areas within the walls were taken up by gardens and monasteries.

The next century witnessed enormous expansion. After the political upheaval of the Dissolution and subsequent Catholic revivals, the stability intro-

Leadenhall market by Ackermann; skins and hides being laid out for drying (Museum of London)

duced by Elizabeth I enabled London to assume the role of Europe's largest port and market. Closer links were forged with Antwerp, Amsterdam and the Baltic League and new imports arrived from America, Africa and the Far East – tobacco, silk, spices and precious metals.

One offspring of this golden age was Sir Thomas Gresham, who in 1571 founded the Royal Exchange. Since the old Roman forum no permanent meeting place for wholesale merchants had existed. Inspired by Antwerp's Bourse, Gresham demolished eighty houses and constructed a grand arcade of shops around a huge quadrangle. It was the largest secular building in London, and a deliberate attempt to place the City ahead of Antwerp as the commercial capital of the world.

London's growth was painstakingly and nostalgically chronicled by John Stow. Within the City walls he saw the gardens of noblemen's houses converted into bowling alleys or built on for merchants' houses. London attracted new indust-

ries employing pewterers, cutlers, glassblowers and jewellers, refining imported materials. By 1600 London's population had reached 200,000. The City was bursting at the seams. The markets of Cheapside, the Stocks, Leadenhall, Billingsgate, Cornhill and the Shambles grew busier, rowdier and more congested, and beyond the walls new suburbs were developing around the markets at Smithfield and Borough High Street. Obnoxious industries like brewing, tanning and brickfiring were exiled to Southwark, Bermondsey, Clerkenwell and Shoreditch. Unseemly pleasures were also banished from the City, prostitutes being confined to the stews at Southwark and Cock Lane in Smithfield.

By the time Stow died in 1605 the fields he knew as a boy were covered by houses and taverns. Old country lanes had become lined with tenements and new markets were taking root in Whitecross Street and Leather Lane, overspill for the crowded markets within the City.

Stuart and Georgian Growth

Meteoric expansion continued in the seventeenth century. By 1660 London boasted 400,000 inhabitants. Within the City walls population was stable but the parishes outside such as Clerkenwell, Whitechapel, Shoreditch and Holborn experienced huge increases. London was still fed largely by the surrounding counties but the sheer size of the City now drew produce from further afield – cheese from Yorkshire, cattle from the West Country, sheep from Norfolk. Bulky fodder and hay was supplied locally, perishable milk and butter came from the pastures and dairy herds of Islington and Essex, and on the hills of Greenwich, Islington and Highgate windmills ground corn to make bread flour.

At the daily food markets of Newgate, Cheapside, Leadenhall and, outside the walls, Whitecross Street and Leather Lane, country produce was sold direct from farmer to housewife. Although numerous permanent shops were now competing, market stalls were traditionally cheaper for retail food. Some of the small medieval street markets could no longer cope with demand or congestion. The Bread Street market was replaced by large bakeries in Southwark where massive ovens produced bread for distribution all over London.

The Great Fire of 1666 wiped out the medieval city. Following the Great Plague of the previous year which had killed 110,000 Londoners, the devastation of the Fire provided the opportunity to reorganize London. The most immediate change was that the suburbs, generally undamaged by the Fire, took on more importance. For the first few years thousands of homeless Londoners camped out in the fields, and many chose not to return to live within the City walls, but to start again outside.

Between 1670 and 1690 London was seized by a vast property boom, mainly in the Strand, Soho and Piccadilly areas, previously fields, woods and gardens. The name Soho derives from a hunting cry, 'So-Ho!'. Inigo Jones's Piazza at Covent Garden had shown the way, back in 1631.

Among new streets of housing markets quickly sprang up, reinforced by an Act of Parliament in 1674 which banned street markets within the City. After the disastrous experience of the Fire open

The Shambles market at Newgate near Paternoster Square (Museum of London)

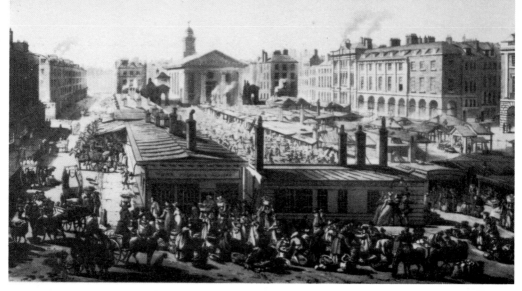

Inigo Jones's Covent Garden piazza, cluttered with wooden shacks and stalls – Pugin and Rowlandson (G.L.C.)

stalls and stands cluttering the narrow streets were regarded as a dangerous nuisance. The old markets of Cheapside, Lime Street, Gracechurch Street and Honey Lane closed. Within the City Leadenhall, Newgate, Billingsgate and the Stocks markets were rebuilt as covered markets under charters granted by Charles II. The Merry Monarch was kept busy throughout his reign authorizing new markets, filling the wearisome gaps between visits from Nell Gwynne.

Outside the City the Earl of Clare owned the land south of Lincoln's Inn Fields to the Strand and in 1657 laid out a street and a market for 'both flesh and fish, bearing his name'. Clare market prospered after the Fire and became noted for pork. A fragment of the old street survives south of Portsmouth and Portugal Streets, hemmed in by the modern London School of Economics. The market was swept away for the Aldwych–Kingsway scheme in 1900. The Old Curiosity Shop was preserved – in Stuart times it was a dairy, later a bookbinding business with which Dickens dealt.

In 1670 the Earl of Bedford was granted a charter to hold a market for fruit, vegetables and herbs in the middle of the piazza at Covent Garden. Such was the success of this market that its wooden sheds, stalls and wagons laden with country produce soon overwhelmed the smart residential character of the Piazza. Inigo Jones was not alive to protest. Nearby

on the south side of the Strand Sir Edward Hungerford opened a market for meat, fish and vegetables in 1680, though it suffered somewhat from the proximity of Covent Garden.

Landowners quickly jumped on the bandwagon, keen to earn revenue from their estates by establishing markets. Henry Jermyn, who had acquired fields next to St James's Palace, erected St James's market in 1680, very close to where Piccadilly Circus is now. Mr Wall started making sausages in St James's market from where he secured the supreme honour of supplying King George I. Later Nash cleared it away to build Regent Street. Berwick Street, Soho, Strutton Ground, Westminster and Newport market, near Leicester Square, were all developed in the 1680s, followed by Carnaby market (where Liberty's stands today) in 1690.

North of the City Spitalfields, formerly belonging to St Mary's Hospital, was colonized by Huguenot refugees, highly skilled in silkweaving, glassblowing and delft pottery. A general food market was established for their convenience in 1682 in Spital Square.

The City fathers viewed the new suburban markets with dismay. Here was a direct challenge to the long-established supremacy of the City markets which gave them their power and wealth. Under medieval doctrine the City authorities held a legal monopoly over all markets within a radius of six and two thirds miles of the City (possibly based on the distance one could reasonably walk from home to market and back in a day). The City Corporation fiercely opposed applications for new markets, and objected bitterly to the cattle and hay markets which sprang up at Knightsbridge and White-chapel. Medieval regulations had been designed to protect buyers from the corrupt practices of 'forestalling' and 'regrating', where dealers bought goods outside a legal market and resold at a profit, or bought at one market and resold at another. Cattle forestallers saved the drover and herdsman the longer and irksome journey to Smithfield and the official salesman's fees and tolls.

The City successfully thwarted a market licence at Knightsbridge but they could not stamp out unofficial trading. Clandestine dealing undermined the City's principles of open market and, as the suburbs grew, markets set up wherever buyer and seller could conveniently gather. Sometimes the City turned a blind eye, as with the markets at Hoxton and Shadwell which 'lie remote from any other'. Although the City prevented a new cattle market at Hounslow, their opposition was increas-ingly overruled. In 1692 Lord Brooke successfully fought their objections and opened Brooke market, a small meat market near Leather Lane. Gradually the case for new local markets was conceded.

What had started in the 1670s carried on apace in the eighteenth century. The Georgian era produced grand estate developments, each carefully planned with formal squares, churches and markets as integral components. Shepherd Market in Mayfair was typical. The old May Fair, held on meadows next to the Tyburn river, had degenerated into a debauched and licentious carnival, attracting hooligans and troublemakers. It was banned in 1708, and in 1735 the land was covered with respectable residences by Edward Shepherd, in-cluding a genteel provisions market for 'flesh, fish, fowl, roots and herbs'. The bawdy Half Moon Inn in Piccadilly was cleared.

Edward Harley, Duke of Portland, duly included a market in his Marylebone estate, the building imparting a country-town character with steep roof, cupola and weathervane. The Oxford market opened in 1731, despite opposition from the owners of the Carnaby market, and lasted until 1880. Market Place today is tucked behind C. & A.'s near

The Haymarket in 1800. The columned portico is still a familiar landmark (G.L.C.)

Oxford Circus. The triangular Grosvenor market off South Molton Street similarly served the Grosvenor estate. Mortimer market, today an inconspicuous backwater off Tottenham Court Road near Heal's, was established in 1768 by Hans Winthrop Mortimer who bought the home field of Capper Farm. It survived as a local open-air food market until the University of London expanded in the 1930s.

London's bulkiest requirement was hay to feed the thousands of horses which were the mainstay of the transport system. By 1700 Smithfield was so congested with livestock that it had no room to sell large quantities of hay. The small hay markets in Broadwick Street off Berwick Street and Broad Street near Strutton Ground closed in the 1720s, though the roads retained their breadth. The Haymarket in Piccadilly took over as the main equine refuelling depot; held every Tuesday, Thursday and Saturday, it handled 1,300 carts each day, serving the whole of the West End while Whitechapel catered for the City and East End. The filth of the Haymarket made it one of the most sordid parts of London – hard to believe if you visit the Design Centre today.

Houndsditch remained the market for second-hand clothes. Clothier Street and Exchange Yard, where Cutler Street gold market recently died, was augmented by Rosemary Lane near the Tower. By the 1750s the Jews were also trading in Petticoat Lane, pushing out the Huguenot weavers. At Bermondsey and St John Street, Clerkenwell, obnoxious skin markets flourished, the over-powering reek of the fellmongers pervading the neighbourhood.

In the City the Stocks market was demolished in 1739 to make room for the new Mansion House, residence of the Lord Mayor. The Fleet market in Farringdon Street was supposed to replace it, but most of the fruit and vegetable trade went to Spitalfields. Public access to Billingsgate (fish and coal), Bear Quay and Queenshythe (corn) and Smithfield (cattle), became restricted to wholesale. The medieval policy of market overt had been overwhelmed by economic pressure. Only Leadenhall, Honey Lane and Newgate remained as retail markets within the City. Certain trades still congregated in small districts, like the booksellers around St Paul's Cathedral, but less so than before.

In 1760 Bear Quay and Queenshythe were replaced by the Corn Exchange in Mark Lane which increasingly became a sample market. The City's role was changing from a marketplace handling goods to a financial centre making paper transactions in numerous commodities. The Stock Exchange, founded in a coffee house, began a business in 1773 on which the City still focuses.

Imports flooded into London – Virginian tobacco, West Indian sugar, Canadian beaver fur, Ceylon tea and African spices. New turnpike roads

The Stocks Market, cleared in 1739 for the Mansion House (G.L.C.)

The Corn Exchange, Mark Lane, opened in 1760 (Guildhall Library)

Hogarth's satirical view of Southwark Fair, a carnival of debauchery (Museum of London)

revolutionized communications within Britain, reinforcing London's dominance. By 1750 London's population was 670,000; it was a huge consumer market with more wealth and expectations than ever before. Even in the famine years of 1725, 1740 and 1775 London's markets were always well supplied and escaped the provincial food riots.

Luxury shops selling gloves, wine, perfumes and jewels flourished in the Royal Exchange. In the seventeenth century it had been augmented by the New or Middle Exchange in the Strand but, as the West End became firmly established with its own high-class shops, the Middle Exchange declined. By 1737 it was a haunt of prostitutes and ne'er-do-wells, known as the 'Whores' Nest'.

At the other end of the social scale, fairs were immensely popular. May Fair had been suppressed because of its drunkenness and fornication, but Bartholomew Fair and Southwark Fair carried on, bigger and rougher than ever. Southwark was the largest and longest, held for two weeks every September, until it too was closed in 1762 due to violent disorder. Hogarth's pictorial commentaries were shaped from his solitary wanderings round London's crowded fairgrounds and markets. The gallows at Tyburn were the main venue for public hangings and dozens of sideshows accompanied execution days. Fairs flourished at Greenwich, Hampstead and Horn Fair, south of Rotherhithe.

Most remarkable were the Frost Fairs on the

Part One   The Development of London's Markets

Thames. In December 1683 the river froze from bank to bank and the cold spell continued through into January. Skating and football matches were soon augmented by rows of booths and stalls. John Evelyn remarked, 'There were divers shops of wares quite across as in town. Coaches plied from Westminster to the Temple, and from several other stairs to and fro, as in the streets – it seemed to be a bacchanalian triumph, a carnival on the water.'

The mini Ice Age produced prolonged hard winters again in 1698 and 1740, when oxen were roasted on the ice. One year a sudden thaw carried the fairground booths downstream on the melting floes before their owners could rescue them. In 1825 work began on a new London Bridge with wider arches, and when the old bridge was demolished in 1832 the Thames flowed more freely and never froze again so solidly.

By 1800 London had spread beyond the New Road (Euston Road) to Pentonville, Islington and Camden Town, and south of the river on to Lambeth marshes. The City remained a medieval bastion of privilege, clinging on to its ancient market rights. Billingsgate had a monopoly in fish, and also imported vast tonnages of coal, carried by collier up the Thames or by barge via the new canals. In 1805 London consumed 150,000 cattle and 1,000,000 sheep, nearly all handled by Smithfield, and disgruntled murmurs mounted that it was no longer a suitable location. It was a popular jest in the 1790s to dispose of an unsatisfactory wife at the cattle market. Many other markets were straining under the pressure of inadequate space or poor facilities. Customers included traders buying wares to hawk round the streets from individual carts.

A new age of industrial mechanization, technological innovation and engineering accomplishment was looming. London had grown as big as any city could practically do when limited to the horse for transport. The railways changed all that.

The Frost Fair, December 1683, looking towards London Bridge; an extraordinary scene of skating, sledging, bear-baiting and fairground booths (G.L.C.)

The Railway Era

The steam age revolutionized London's markets. The speed of railway transport enabled produce to be brought twice as far and twice as fast. Dodd remarked in his treatise in 1858, 'Double the speed and you increase four-fold the area of country from whence provisions can be sent in a given time to London.'

Rapid transit was particularly welcome for perishable goods. Previously, fresh meat had to be transported on the hoof which wasted the livestock. Steamships and railways saved the animals the exhausting journeys; furthermore livestock could be killed in the country and the dead meat brought quickly to London. The Thames and North Sea had traditionally supplied London with fish; now railways brought fish from Yarmouth, Grimsby, Fleetwood and Ireland, lobsters from Scotland, oysters from the Channel Islands. Fresh fish had been almost unknown in inland towns like Birmingham before the railways. The suburban cowkeepers who had distributed milk to houses in ten-gallon tubs slung across the shoulders were gradually done out of a job by the railways.

Improvements in the quantity and quality of produce reaching London allowed the markets to keep pace with the march of bricks and mortar as suburbs sprawled out in all directions. Jews, persecuted in Europe and Russia, streamed into the East End at the rate of 4,000 a year, together with Irish labourers escaping domestic famine. Elementary improvements in sanitation and medical care reduced infant mortality and London's population rocketed.

The original intention had been to have one large central railway terminus at Charing Cross. Instead the individual railway companies built their own stations – the first by London, Midland and Scottish in 1837 at Euston, the last at Marylebone in 1899. The distance of the termini from the existing London markets prompted the establishment of new railhead markets.

The London and North East Railway Company which had built King's Cross station in 1850 opened the King's Cross potato market in 1865, supplanting the congested potato market at Tooley Street beside Borough market. A sum of £40,000 was spent on covering four acres west of York Way with thirty-nine warehouses alongside the 'ten o'clock road' railway sidings. The L.N.E.R. offered new hinterlands and within a year the market handled 85,000 tons of Lincolnshire, Yorkshire, Cambridgeshire and Scottish potatoes. Eighty trucks arrived daily and trading was from 5 a.m. to 4 p.m. The wholesalers paid peppercorn rents – the L.N.E.R. regarded the freight as adequate recompense.

In season, King's Cross was a major market for rhubarb, green peas and celery whose two varieties, Blackland and Siltland, came mainly from Huntingdon, Cambridge and West Norfolk. Many street sellers specialized in celery and rhubarb, such was their popularity. It was also the railhead for north-east and Scottish fish, bound for Billingsgate. The City Corporation's monopoly prevented a rival fish market, although it would probably have done rather better than the doomed Shadwell fish market.

Stratford market, built by Great Eastern in 1879, provided a new wholesale outlet for fruit and vegetables for the East End and similar markets opened at Bricklayers Arms off the Old Kent Road and Portman market, Paddington. The Midland Railway arrived in 1866, invading St Pancras churchyard on its way. Next to Gilbert Scott's magnificent station and hotel the company founded the Somers Town market in 1892. The fifteen-acre goods depot, bordered by Euston Road, Midland Road, Phoenix Road and Ossulston Street, swept away the unsavoury slums of Agar Town, infested with knackers' yards, soapworks, bone-boilers and manure-makers. The Brill market disappeared too, with its bird fanciers and wretched child beggars. Besides the railway, smoke belched from brick kilns and mephitic dampness flowed from the gasworks, choking the air with poison and depositing a thick scum of grime. From the elevated tracks goods were lowered into the market by hydraulic lift for grading and sorting. At its peak Somers Town market received 75,000 tons of vegetables per year, mainly potatoes, cabbages, carrots and lettuces.

Somers Town and King's Cross markets died

The Caledonian cattle market, opened in 1855 to replace Smithfield. The tower and railings survive (G.L.C.)

with the Beeching axe. The empty sites now host the new British Library and proposals for vast new office blocks. Only Stratford market survives. Brentford market, opened in 1893 near Kew Bridge by one of the Rothschilds on behalf of Brentford Urban District Council and extended in 1905, was converted into a general retail market in 1974 until that also closed. For a while the huge structure was piled high with scrap cars. Now it has been rebuilt. The wholesale fruit and vegetable market moved to Western International beside the M4 at Heston, modern, spacious, ugly, a small version of New Covent Garden.

The increasing volume of foodstuffs arriving in London necessitated the rebuilding of the older wholesale markets. The ramshackle timber sheds in Covent Garden were replaced in 1830 by an elegant market hall. The railhead markets at King's Cross, Stratford and Somers Town did not stop Covent Garden's inexorable expansion and further buildings were added in 1860 and 1871. The architect, Charles Fowler, was also commissioned to rebuild Hungerford market in 1833, comprising a two-storey hall – fish and meat beside the mists and odours of the river, fruit and luxuries on the upper level. Gilbert Scott worked here as a young trainee during construction. Hungerford footbridge was built in 1854 to encourage south-bank shoppers to use the market, but within ten years the market had gone, replaced by Charing Cross station and hotel.

The City Corporation were quick to see the threat and opportunities posed by railways and poured money into modernizing their markets. Billingsgate was rebuilt by James Bunning in 1852 and enlarged in 1875 by Horace Jones who also reconstructed ancient Leadenhall six years later.

The City's greatest headache involved the Smithfield livestock and Newgate butchers' markets. Eighteenth-century mutterings had escalated into loud and caustic criticism: central London was no place for the sale of live animals or their mass slaughter. But the Corporation obstinately clung to their powers and profits. John Perkins's alternative livestock market off Essex Road, Islington, failed in competition and shut in 1836 with the loss of £100,000. Rivalry was no solution; first Smithfield had to be closed. This was achieved by the Smithfield Market Removal Act in 1852. Three years later Prince Albert opened the Caledonian cattle market on a spacious site at Copenhagen Fields, north Islington. Even by 1849 over half the two million animals reaching London came by rail. The King's Cross line conveniently flanked the new cattle market which flourished up to the Second World War. It finally petered out in 1963, leaving its grand clocktower and market taverns as strange relics.

The chance was grasped to clear the squalid

slaughterhouses and congested stalls of Newgate Shambles, a labyrinth of abattoirs and shops behind Newgate prison. Conditions were appalling; Warwick Lane was only ten feet wide, largely unaltered since the twelfth century but more crowded. The maze of courts and alleys was redeveloped as Paternoster Square, much to the relief of the long-suffering booksellers near St Paul's.

At Smithfield a new dead-meat market was constructed between 1866 and 1868. The decision to build at Smithfield was motivated by the Metropolitan underground railway. Opened in 1863, this linked the Great Western, North Western and Great Northern railway with the City. In 1865 it was extended to Moorgate and joined to the Chatham and Dover line via Holborn and Blackfriars. The Corporation willingly contributed to the cost of the works, which was hardly surprising as it enabled Smithfield to be a railway market. Horace Jones's masterful design located the buildings above the tracks so that meat could be hauled directly into the market.

The success of Smithfield and the Caledonian cattle market persuaded the authorities to terminate Newport market at Leicester Square and crack down on the insalubrious abattoirs in Whitechapel. Shaftesbury Avenue, built by the Metropolitan Board of Works in 1886, and the Palace Theatre at Cambridge Circus removed the last vestige of Newport market. During the nineteenth century nearly every existing market in London was either improved or discontinued. A Guildhall committee in 1869 noted the declining fortunes of Clare, Grosvenor, Oxford and Carnaby markets. They were all demolished by 1900, for road improvements or redevelopment. Spitalfields, Borough and Greenwich wholesale markets were all rebuilt on their original or expanded sites. The Haymarket had become too congested for its surroundings; moreover it was incompatible with the elegance of Nash's inspired scheme for Regent Street and Carlton House Terrace. In 1830 it was moved to the new Cumberland market on the east side of Regent's Park. The hay market lasted here until 1939; the site is now a playground. Tattersall's thoroughbred horse market, originally at Hyde Park Corner, occupied new auction rooms in Knightsbridge in 1865 where it too survived until

The Oxford market near Oxford Circus, 1895, shortly before demolition (Westminster Library)

The Coal Exchange in 1960, sadly demolished for road widening opposite Billingsgate (Guildhall Library)

the Second World War. The entrance gates were re-erected at Newmarket. Aldridge's in St Martin's Lane switched from horses to cars in 1926.

The square mile of the City remained the hub of commerce and finance. The Commercial Sale Rooms were established in Mincing Lane in 1811 as the central market dealing in imports such as rubber, ivory, hemp, silk and jute. Tea, coffee, sugar and cocoa were sampled and tasted while the bulk was held for distribution in vast warehouses beside St Katharine's Dock and Royal Victoria Dock. Silk and ostrich feathers, sprayed with naphthalene preservative, were kept at Houndsditch. The Mincing Lane premises were enlarged in 1890; now they may move to old Billingsgate.

Forty acres of warehousing in the docks were devoted to storing and exhibiting Australian and New Zealand wool. Experts inspected the cargoes by tearing bunches from the bulging bales and then rushed to the City to bargain in the Wool Exchange in Coleman Street.

The industrial revolution, and the railways in particular, depended on coal. James Bunning's Coal Exchange, opened in 1849, was a glorious testament to its importance, a magnificent edifice with central rotunda and glazed dome, four storeys high. It stood in Lower Thames Street opposite Billingsgate until it was tragically and senselessly demolished in 1962. The Corn Exchange in Mark Lane was enlarged twice between 1850 and 1880. The Royal Exchange, Bank of England and Stock Exchange were all rebuilt to cater for those boom days of the Empire.

The wealth of the City Corporation and the individual merchants, deriving from the phenomenal prosperity of their markets, bred numerous acts of philanthropy. One of the most celebrated was the Columbia market, designed in extravagant gothic splendour to afford protection and facilities for the impoverished street traders of east London. Randall's market in Poplar, erected in 1850 by Onisophodros Randall and demolished in 1930, was a similar venture. Amid the affluence of the railway age, the colossal investment in new and old wholesale markets and grandiose Victorian buildings, here was recognition, albeit misguided, of the existence and poverty of the bottom rung of the market ladder, the humble street seller.

Victorian Street Sellers

Estimates of the numbers of street sellers in Victorian London vary. By 1900 there were probably 60,000, of whom at least half were traditional costermongers selling fruit, vegetables and fish. During the week they roamed the streets but on Saturdays and Sundays congregated into huge markets in the poor parts of London when the workers did their shopping.

Costermongers were originally apple-sellers. The costard was an indigenous variety of apple, large and sour, which flourished in England before the sophisticated hybrids bred during the eighteenth century. A costard tree stands in Kew Gardens on the lawn in front of the Queen's Cottage. In time the term costermonger was applied to all manner of street sellers.

The art of hawking and peddling is as old as any but in Victorian London it boomed as never before or since. The poor bought their food, clothes and minor luxuries in the street from the barrows, carts and baskets of hucksters and costers. Half the fruit and veg. at Covent Garden and three quarters of Billingsgate's fish were bought directly by street traders who then distributed their wares round the poor residential districts.

It was a desperately hard way of scraping a living, but one that many resorted to through lack of any obvious alternative. London's streets were supposedly paved with gold and many went in search of it. Costers usually worked sixteen hours every day, living from hand to mouth, their faces tired, drawn and pinched. Children were thrown into the fray to fend for themselves at the age of six or seven, and elderly street sellers struggled on until winter frosts gripped their wheezing chest or the workhouse took them in. Costermongers were at the mercy of the weather; heavy rain deterred custom, heatwaves rotted the fish and fruit, the cold crippled them. Many were too poor to own their barrows and exorbitant hire charges ensnared them in a hopeless poverty trap.

Almost anything could be bought on the street from the multitude of specialist hawkers. For food there were piemen, hot-eel boys, rhubarb-sellers, old men with trays of cough-drops, milk-sellers, watercress girls, the hot-potato vendor – 'keep your 'ands warm while you eat 'em' – sellers of pickled whelks and sheep's trotters. Jewish orange wenches, 'handsome nut brown dark-haired daughters of Israel, jewelled and ribboned', bought their sup-

Selling firewood in a Walworth backstreet, 1887 (Southwark Library)

Mrs Grant in Skipton Street, Elephant and Castle, 1890 (Southwark Library)

plies in the Duke's Place orange mart near Aldgate, and then walked for hours to sell their basketload. The Irish cats' meat man was followed like the Pied Piper by every cat in the neighbourhood, while on Sunday afternoons the muffin man with his insistent bell trudged round smarter suburbs.

Umpteen petty traders plied the streets offering services – scissors to mend, knives to grind (using treadle-operated whetstones), lavender, buttons and bouquets of primroses. Hearthstone-sellers, match boys, coal men, shoe-blackers and street-crossing sweepers all tried their luck. Others scratched or begged a living as entertainers – acrobats, conjurers, strongmen, snake-swallowers, mice-exhibitors and penny-gaff clowns.

Despite being indispensable to the shopping needs of the poor, street sellers were perpetually at war with the police and local authorities. Costers were regarded as the main reason for traffic congestion. Frequently moved on, charged with obstruction or dispossessed of their barrows, the costers were buffeted from pillar to post. As a result they became a closer knit community than any other contemporary workforce.

In 1875 the Public Health Act introduced the first legislation aimed at controlling street markets, the spacing of stalls and street-cleaning. Barrows were to be single file, three feet apart and not obstructing the breadth of the street by more than the width of one cart. Stepney Borough Council ordered in 1904 that 'no person shall at any time between the hours of midnight and six in the morning or at any time on Sunday for the purpose of hawking, selling, distributing or advertising any article make any violent outcry or noise in any street or public place so as to cause annoyance to the inhabitants of the neighbourhood', on pain of a forty-shilling fine. The police could prosecute, but many street markets were unauthorized until 1927 when the London County Council at last tightened the licensing and control of street trading and introduced stricter sanitation rules.

Friday and Saturday evenings and Sunday morning were the busiest times for costermongers. Friday was payday for labourers and servants; street sellers clustered together to form enormous markets in working-class areas. Mayhew, in 1849, knew of fifteen Sunday morning markets in central London, mostly in the East End where the Jewish markets in Petticoat Lane, Whitechapel, and Brick Lane came to life after the silent Saturday sabbath. The Christian Church and the respectable middle classes fervently opposed the Sunday markets and the disrespect for the hours of divine worship.

The New Cut on Christmas morning; the police stay in pairs (G.L.C.)

The liveliest and wildest Saturday night markets were the Brill at Somers Town, Lambeth Walk, the New Cut and East Street. Trading continued beyond midnight into the early hours. Thousands of people spent the whole evening under the naphtha oil lamps looking for bargains and enjoying the fun of the fair. Every type of street seller and entertainer was present, and every form of Victorian diversion; this was the night to make a bob. Quack doctors exhibited diagrams of the intestines or warts which their nostrums had cured; next to machines for trying strength or testing the power of the lungs, makeshift dentists drew decayed teeth; for the price of a penny the perky love-birds of Romany fortune tellers picked fortune cards from a rack beside their perch; monkeys tethered to Italian organ-grinders begged for money; cheapjacks sold 'Turkish rhubarb' made of dahlia tubers dyed with saffron; bird fanciers displayed their unhappy linnets, deprived of native woodland; and fishmongers exhibited mackerel whose lustreless skin suggested a lengthy absence from the sea. Women in black shawls haggled for yesterday's cabbages or hunted through scraggy pieces of meat seeking some humble luxury for the family dinner; cigars, toffees, watercress, trinkets and perfumed wallflowers tempted the senses and pockets of the passer-by.

Petticoat Lane had replaced the old Rag Fair clothes market. Countless second-hand garments dangled on poles blocking shopfront windows and shutting out the light. At the rougher markets like the Brill and New Cut policemen reconnoitred in pairs, and waifs, strays, pickpockets and tricksters abounded. Stallholders often fought for the best pitches, hence the introduction of the practice of blowing a police whistle as a signal for the costers to race for position.

Street sellers were full of patter and tales of 'shipwrecked' goods. Sometimes a colleague made the first purchase to start the ball rolling. Stock displayed at the front was superior to the goods sold from the back of the stall. Despite competition it was the costers' unwritten convention not to queer another's pitch or to tell his yarn until the next one had finished.

Street cries were part and parcel of the great markets and the lone hawker. The markets generated an indescribable vocal din. Lungs of stentorian power, bawling, squealing, shouting, yelling and hallooing combined into a cacophony of rhythm, pitch and volume. Touts kept up a constant crossfire of noise: 'Come on, my dears, buy at your price tonight' ... 'Ni-ew mackerel, six a shilling' ... 'Collar studs, a penny for two and two a penny' ... 'Hot spiced gingerbread, smokin' hot. If one'll warm you, wha-at'll a pound do?' ... 'Penny a bunch, turnips'.

Smart jokes and repartee were squeezed among the wordy harangue, a tradition very much alive in today's markets, syllables distorted by repetition. 'Eeenglish strawberries, none of yer euro rubbish; 'ere you are, fresh banaanaas, luverly banaanaas, twen'y a pound, pick yer own bunch, darlin'.'

Less apparent now are the cries of the solitary street sellers outside the markets. Cockney counterparts of Sweet Molly Malone wheeled their barrows through the side streets singing: 'Sprats alive, all alive-O'. 'Muffins for tea', 'Matches', and 'Won't you buy my sweet lavender?' were familiar cries. When close, some hawkers competed by the loudness of their yells. Two such hawkers stood outside Sadler's Wells Theatre in the 1890s, one selling whelks, the other boiled pigs' trotters at a halfpenny each. Delectable though their morsels were, it disconcerted an audience – silent with sympathy at the saddest moment as the heroine weeps over the dying Little Willie, 'Dead! and ...

never called me mother' – to hear the booming voice of George Belmont wafting up the gallery stairs, 'Trotters, two a penne-e-e!'

Equally famous was cockney rhyming and back slang developed by the costers to mystify the police who hounded them. 'Esclop' for 'police', or 'Adam and Eve' for 'believe', were part of a secret language which alerted fellows of approaching trouble and baffled suspect strangers.

The more successful Victorian costermongers fashioned a distinctive stylish dress as well as a tough manner and sharp wit. Silk neckerchieves called 'king's men', long cord waistcoats decorated with pearl buttons, a carefully angled cloth cap and brightly polished boots were the mark of the fancy coster. The ceremonial uniforms of pearly kings and queens evolved from the craze of the 1880s for pearl buttons, manufactured from lustrous seashells in scores of East End factories.

Pearly kings and queens were the elite of the coster community, 'monarchies' elected borough by borough who spent their time collecting for charity and Christmas treats for the elderly and destitute

Primrose-seller, 1905; the lot of many young girls (Guildhall Library)

The muffin man, 1900; a common sight in London until the 1920s (Guildhall Library)

Pearly kings and queens parade for harvest festival, Bermondsey, 1930 (Southwark Library)

costers. The City of London pearly king still attends Petticoat Lane every Sunday. The carnival dresses and suits were each covered with up to 30,000 buttons – pride dictated that no cloth should show, the buttons overlapping like fish scales – and sewn in symbolic patterns of faith, hope and charity (cross, anchor and heart). Vivid silk mufflers and brilliant ostrich feathers in their hats embellished this extraordinary regalia, as far removed from the realities of everyday costermongers' attire as the official Life Guards' uniform was from the trenches.

Every October London's pearly kings and queens met for a harvest festival thanksgiving service in the Old Kent Road. The ceremony survives now in St Martin-in-the-Fields, but the turnout is lower and declining. In 1974 only forty-two pearlies were left, the younger generation having shunned tradition. Their annual holiday which included the parade of donkeys, the costers' derby and basket-carrying contests at Crystal Palace has also died out. Donkey carts, once a cheap and dashing way to travel, have disappeared from London's streets.

Street sellers and entertainers flocked to the occasional fairs which attracted enormous crowds. The authorities did their best to suppress the older fairs, where eighteenth-century gambling and depravity offended strict Victorian morals. Battersea Fair had been a popular excursion; 15,000 people landed at the pier and 40,000 came by road. Prize fighters, Punch and Judy, German wind bands, barrel-organs and bearded women amused the crowds while the beer houses provided no less an attraction. In 1846 the local vicar and Thomas Cubitt won their campaign; the fair was closed and a new park laid out landscaped with earth scooped from the excavations for London's docks. Respectable housing replaced the taverns.

Bartholomew Fair was abolished in 1855, as were the old village fairs at Mile End, Bow, Peckham, Harrow, Camberwell, Tottenham Court and Brook Green. Only a few survived: Greenwich Fair, described by Dickens as 'a three-day fever which cools the blood for six months after', and 'appy 'ampstead Fair were boosted by the introduction of Bank Holidays in 1871. The September Barnet horse fair continued beside the railway station until the fields were bought for building.

The majority of London's existing street markets are the direct descendants of markets begun in the first decades of Victoria's reign. A London County

Part One   The Development of London's Markets

Council survey in 1896 noted over one hundred street markets: 'They serve the useful purpose of providing poor and crowded neighbourhoods with cheap surplus produce remaining unsold in the authorized [i.e. wholesale] markets.' Most survived until 1939, and in the thirties there were still over 30,000 costers in London, many ex-servicemen.

Some Victorian markets have disappeared completely. Chalton Street is a pale reflection of the rowdy rabble that inundated the Brill, cleared away for the Somers Town railway market next to St Pancras. Similarly Lower Marsh is a genteel offshoot of the notorious New Cut. Main-road markets at Aldgate, Tottenham Court Road, Caledonian Road, Walworth Road and Camden High Street were removed due to traffic obstruction, particularly when tram tracks were laid in the 1890s. Traders took refuge in side streets like East Street, Inverness Street or Rathbone Street. North End Road and Farringdon Road are unusual examples of markets still operating in busy roads.

With depopulation and redevelopment other Victorian markets declined to the verge of extinc-

tion. The lonely stalls in Salmon Lane (Limehouse), Burdett Road (Mile End), and Devons Road (Bromley-By-Bow) are ghosts of once thriving street markets. Little Earl Street (now Earlham Street) off Seven Dials, where dozens of stalls lined both gutters, has a handful today; Goodge Place has even fewer. Marmont Road (Peckham), Hessel Street (Whitechapel), Albion Street (Rotherhithe) and Norland Road (Fulham) are still designated markets but haven't seen a stall for years.

Shopping patterns shifted. Edwardian department stores – Harrods, Selfridges and Liberty's – flourished in the West End. Chains of grocery shops and then supermarkets conspired against outdoor trading. The era of the music hall was ended abruptly by the cinema. It is surprising that street markets have survived at all in our supermarket age, yet some do more than survive: Brixton, Ridley Road, Leather Lane, Shepherd's Bush and Chapel Market are busier than ever.

Many of the Victorian customs also survive, none more so than the traditional costermongers' barrows, still a familiar sight in London's streets. The

Tottenham Court Road, 1911 (G.L.C.)

skilled craftsmen who repair the wooden carts and hire them out to the traders are born into the trade. Some firms are now in their fourth or fifth generation, like Ellen Keeley who began operating from Covent Garden in 1830. Sadly, Mr Sullivan, the last of the line, moved out of his Neal Street workshop a few years back. In South London, Joe Tappy still hires out from Lambeth Walk, while Hillier and Howard Brothers supply the East End and Smithfield. Sowle and Sons of Bombay Street mend stalls for East Street. The simple design of the coster's barrow is unchanged. Replacement parts for the undercarriage are a problem, and although the metal rims can be replaced nobody makes the traditional wooden wheels now. Gradually, smaller aluminium wheels with rubber tyres are being fixed instead.

Mr Sullivan in his Neal Street workshop, keeping old traditions alive

The Victorian street seller remains a strong influence on the character of London's present-day markets, but nothing is static for very long. In November 1982 Tower Hamlets decided to extinguish the Sunday Club Row market. This notorious East End institution just off Brick Lane began as an unofficial livestock market in the 1670s to avoid Smithfield tolls. In the nineteenth century it was a bird market selling linnets, thrushes and finches to the poor. In the thirties, greyhounds, rabbits, ducks and geese took over. Hen auctions were held in Bell Street off Petticoat Lane. The RSPCA's campaign against ill-treatment of puppies and kittens closed Club Row in the end. The 'boys' or the 'fancy', the unshaven con-men, swindlers and poachers with shifty eyes and rotting teeth, have moved on to new hunting grounds. Memories of song birds and pet monkeys fade into legend and history books.

The Cutler Street gold and silver market in Exchange Buildings Yard and Putney Flea Market have both disappeared as concrete and glass digests more of old London. No doubt others will go too in the future. Car-boot sales are all the rage now, fly-by-nights here today, gone tomorrow. Yet the market boom seems stronger than ever. Gabriel's Wharf, Camden Lock, Earls Court and the new sites for Billingsgate and Spitalfields wholesale markets represent another shake of the kaleidoscope, a further twist in the tale of London's markets. It's a show which will run and run.

Cheshire Street, 1904, part of the Club Row bird market (Tower Hamlets Library)

Part Two

Battersea High Street, SW11

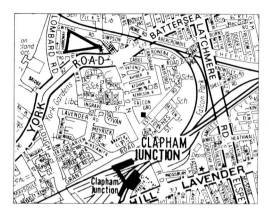

Merchandise: Small food market: wet fish, eggs, fruit and vegetables, flowers, cassettes.

Opening times: 9.00 a.m. to 5.00 p.m. Friday and Saturday.

Location: South end of Battersea High Street, between Battersea Park Road and Simpson Street.

Nearest railway station: Clapham Junction (Victoria, Waterloo).

Buses: Nos. 19, 39, 44, 45, 49, 170 (Battersea Park Road).

Battersea High Street is not the liveliest or busiest market one could wish for as a starter, but is the victim of alphabetical order. The dozen surviving stalls are a sad reflection of massive housing redevelopment over the last twenty years, when the old community was uprooted, the area depopulated and then invaded by yuppies.

Despite all the upheavals, Battersea is a fascinating place. The High Street was the curving spine of a Saxon hamlet which remained a small village until 1835. Battersea's market gardens prospered on the fertile loam soils of the Thames flood plain. After the Dissolution of the Monasteries by Henry VIII the art of kitchen gardening wellnigh disappeared in England; Anne Boleyn had to send abroad for fresh lettuce. Protestant immigrants reintroduced the skills, and one such colony settled in Battersea. Asparagus was grown in England for the first time. By 1800, 200 acres of the parish were devoted to asparagus beds, producing 'Battersea Bundles', the size of rhubarb, each head weighing 4oz. Carrots, onions and radish were grown for seed and supplied Surrey's gardens.

The railway carved a great swathe through Battersea. Between 1850 and 1870 Battersea's fields disappeared under gasworks, breweries, Price's candles, Morgan's crucible factory and cheap workers' housing. Perhaps the High Street market began as the last of the market gardeners sold their produce to the new factory workers. By the 1890s it was well established as a large and popular market, which makes the present even sadder.

Battersea's gentrification has probably prevented the total demise of the market. With the High Street attractively paved and adorned with traditional bollards and Victorian lamp-posts it is now pleasantly traffic-free. Although scores of pitches are optimistically marked out, the market has sensibly contracted to Fridays and Saturdays only. Several stalls do good business. Nearby Simpson Street has been done up, Battersea Park Road is prosperously smart. Perhaps the High Street market will thrive again.

The High Street continues north of the railway. Three pubs, the Woodman, the Original Woodman and the Castle, hint at old village days long past. The Castle, built in 1600, was one of Battersea's oldest inns but was demolished and rebuilt by Young's in 1965. Someone recorded the price of mild on a plaque outside – one farthing per pint in 1660, 1s 5d per pint in 1965. At that rate come 2270 A.D. it will be £4.76 per 57 centilitres!

(*overleaf*) Tachbrook Street

Beresford Square, SE18

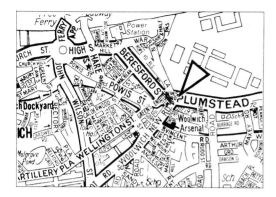

Merchandise: Fruit, vegetables, fish, meat, clothes, flowers, jewellery, hardware.

Opening times: 8.30 a.m. to 5 p.m. Tuesday to Saturday. Half-day closing Thursday.

Location: Beresford Square, Woolwich.

Nearest railway station: Woolwich Arsenal (London Bridge).

Buses: Nos. 51, 53, 96, 99, 122, 161, 177, 180.

Woolwich has had a market since the Middle Ages, held until the Dissolution on church land with tolls going to the Bishop of Rochester. In 1620 James I granted a charter to a local landowner and the market rights remained in private hands until 1887 when the Local Board of Health acquired them from the owner, Sir Spencer Maryon Wilson.

Initially the market had operated in the High Street and Market Hill beside the river-ferry landing-stage. During the nineteenth century Royal Dockyard expansion and the munitions factory saw the ancient parishes of Woolwich, Charlton and Plumstead enveloped in artisans' housing. The market stallholders moved from Market Hill to the square outside the main gates of the Royal Arsenal through which thousands of men and women trudged to work each day. Nobody enters the Royal Arsenal today but outside the dignified gateway, built in 1829 (its clock still goes), the Beresford Square market thrives.

The compactness of the stalls is akin to a provincial market square rather than a straggling street market. Run by locals for the locals, several families have monopolized affairs for over a century – the Hicks, Manchesters, Ellises, Delieus, Edwards, Denards and Rolfes. Stalls are jealously kept in the family, although the Council has tried to stop patriarchal nominations. Stability has bred longevity; Albert Manchester sold fruit in Beresford Square for over seventy years, and served in the Great War.

The ninety stalls provide remarkable choice and quality. Fruit and vegetables, like Delieu's bananas, are reliable, the fish stall excellent; lampshades, football souvenirs, clothes pegs, pop records, Hoover attachments, silk scarves, flowers and pet food add to the medley. Near by on the south side of Plumstead Road the Council also runs the covered market, open every day except Thursday and Sunday. Apart from the butcher by the pavement, most of the fifty-eight permanent kiosks sell durables such as clothes and carpets. But traffic races past the dingy entrance and the open square has more atmosphere and freshness. Trams used to plough through the middle of the market irritating costers, customers and passengers.

For refreshment try the eel, mash and pie café in Woolwich New Road or the Tramshed further along. Actually in Beresford Square the Ordnance has had a hideous pub front stuck on to a splendid Victorian corner building. Beresford Square market is the best thing left in Woolwich. One suspects that many Highbury residents would happily swop it for Arsenal Football Club.

Berwick Street, W1

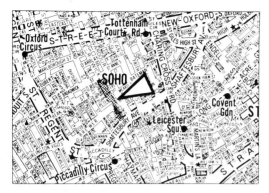

Merchandise: Mainly food, wide range of fruit and vegetables, some clothing and fabrics.

Opening times: 9 a.m. to 5 p.m. Monday to Saturday.

Location: Berwick Street, south of Broadwick Street, extending into Rupert Street.

Nearest tube: Oxford Circus (Victoria, Central), Piccadilly Circus (Bakerloo, Piccadilly), Tottenham Court Road (Northern).

Buses: Nos. 7, 8, 25, 73, 176 (Oxford Street), nos. 14, 19, 22, 38 (Shaftesbury Avenue).

This is the friendliest street in Soho, one of the delights of the West End, and a welcome refuge from so much garishness and artificiality. Coming from Oxford Street the daily market begins at Broadwick Street; from here on the narrow road becomes confined with stalls and barrows. At its busiest at lunchtimes, the pedestrian throng clogs the street; traffic is out of the question and is rightly banned.

Berwick Street was built between 1688 and 1689, a time of religious turmoil, and named by a papist to honour the Duke of Berwick, the young illegitimate son of James II who was fighting to restore his father's throne. Off Berwick Street the width of Broadwick Street accommodated a hay market, while gunpowder was manufactured in Peter Street from salt petre. Berwick Street market began in the 1840s when Soho had become densely populated – almost entirely by labouring classes, notably Italian and Jewish tailors. When the old Monmouth market near Seven Dials was closed down for the building of Shaftesbury Avenue many stallholders moved to an expanding Berwick Street market.

Thousands of artisans lived above shops and workrooms in dingy lodgings and it was here that the ghastly London cholera epidemic of 1854 broke out. By plotting the deaths on a map, Dr John Snow was the first conclusively to link cholera with drinking water, in this case a contaminated pump in Broadwick Street. Previously it had been believed that cholera was spread by 'miasma', the polluted air of graveyards and sewers. Forty years later there was still a ban on selling any goods in the market which might spread contagion, such as second-hand clothes.

By the 1930s the market's character had changed. Despite its reputation for London's most pressing stall sellers, it was renowned for its chintzes, satin remnants, furs, and fine silk stockings, popular with chorus girls from theatreland. The area breathed show-biz. Jessie Matthews (Mrs Dale) was born at No. 94 Berwick Street; her father had a stall in the market. It was one of the first street markets to use electric lights, with plugs installed in the pavement walls. Other markets in the thirties relied on oil lamps which needed constant trimming and polishing to woo them into giving light.

Since the war Oxford Street's department stores have taken most of the millinery trade from Berwick Street, and now it is best for its food, particularly its variety of exotic fruit and vegetables: mangoes, shaddocks, passion fruit, lychees, avocado pears and aubergines. Berwick Street was the first street market to sell unusual fruit, perhaps because it has always had a sprinkling of upper-class customers (one stallholder used to supply King Edward VII with pears). Jack Smith, a Berwick Street trader for sixty years, was the first to sell tomatoes on a London street in 1880 and, in 1890, the first to sell grapefruit. A new consignment had arrived at Middlesex Wharf in Wapping which traders avoided with suspicion. Three days later they still sat unsold. Jack bought the lot at one shilling a case, sold them at Berwick Street and made £250!

Berwick Street has great character even though the old buildings are left on only one side of the street. The crowds are a cosmopolitan mixture of locals, actors, office workers, strippers, tourists.

Don't miss Camisa's at No. 1a Berwick Street. Ennio Camisa has lived in Soho for sixty years and since 1944 Camisa and his son Alberto have run their Berwick Street shop, making their own delicious pasta and selling a fantastic range of cheeses – an attraction in its own right. At No. 84 is Kopelovitch's lace shop, which sells the best lace in London. The Algerian Coffee Stores in Old Compton Street offer superb quality, and Lina Stores in Brewer Street rivals Camisa as a first-class Italian grocer. The local Jewish tradition still survives at Joelson's, 28 Peter Street, which sells all the Hebrew delicacies. Cranks Health Food Shop and restaurant in Marshall Street is more recent, but nonetheless excellent – a welcome oasis after the glitter and tat of Carnaby Street.

Bethnal Green Road, E2

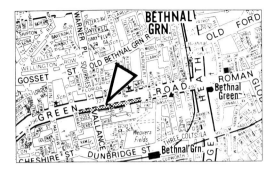

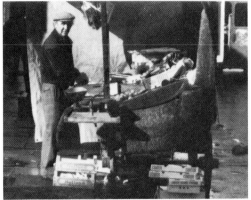

Merchandise: Mainly food, household goods.

Opening times: 8.30 a.m. to 5 p.m. Monday to Saturday. Half-day closing Thursday.

Location: South side of Bethnal Green Road between Vallance Road and Wilmot Street.

Nearest tube: Bethnal Green (Central).

Buses: Nos. 8, 8A.

On Fridays and Saturdays this is a good general street market. About eighty closely packed stalls line the south side of Bethnal Green Road selling fruit and veg., fish, packaged and tinned food and general household goods. During the rest of the week only a few stallholders bother to set up and the market is a rather sparse and straggling affair.

Nobody travels far to come here: it is very much for locals, as it has been for at least a hundred and fifty years. In 1833 a petition from residents of the parish of St Matthew, Bethnal Green, complained about the incursion of the market into residential side streets and objected to the depraved language and behaviour of the Sunday crowds. The market no longer operates on Sundays, although the Sunday morning clamour and uproar of Brick Lane and Club Row are not far away.

Bethnal Green Road is a drab and shabby street, which is nothing new. Matthew Arnold described it over a century ago:

'Twas August, and the fierce sun overhead
Smote on the squalid streets of Bethnal Green,
And the pale weaver, through his windows seen
In Spitalfields, look'd thrice dispirited . . .

Silkweaving, brought to Bethnal Green and

Spitalfields by Huguenot refugees, has long since died out as a local industry.

The Green itself is refreshingly pleasant with the church of St John and St Bartholomew and the Bethnal Green Museum next to it. This is a lovely building inside, not unlike a Victorian markethall, built originally for the 1851 Exhibition and re-erected in 1872 at Bethnal Green as a branch of the V. & A.

The museum is well known for its collection of clothes as worn by both the ruling and working classes over the centuries, and for its locally woven silk calico, dating from the 1670s. Rodin donated a large group of his sculptures. Best for kids is the display of toys, dolls' houses and puppets, a Georgian and Victorian Hamleys.

Brick Lane, E1 and E2

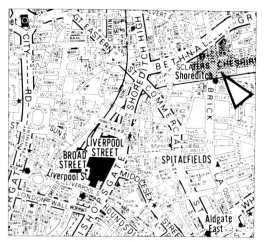

Merchandise: A huge variety of new and second-hand goods, including clothes, furniture, carpets, electrical equipment, tools, shoes, bicycles, fresh and packaged food.

Opening times: Daybreak to midday Sunday.

Location: Brick Lane, north of the railway bridge up to Bethnal Green Road, Cheshire Street, Cygnet Street, Bacon Street, Sclater Street, Chilton Street.

Nearest tube: Liverpool Street (Metropolitan, Circle), Aldgate East (District), Old Street (Northern).

Buses: No. 8 (Bethnal Green Road), nos. 5, 22A, 67 (Commercial Street), nos. 6, 22, 35, 47, 48, 55, 78, 149, 243, 263 (Shoreditch High Street).

Sunday morning at Brick Lane is probably the most genuine survivor in London of a market for the poor and the working classes. Brick Lane is a must for any seasoned market-goer; its atmosphere is unique, the prices are miraculously cheap – but expect no gentility. The market clogs the north part of Brick Lane, and also fills many of the side streets, particularly Cheshire Street. Many goods are second hand, sold from sheds, shacks, barrows, upturned milk crates or outstretched palms.

The eastern end of Cheshire Street is one of the more depressing sights of London. Here are sad rows of old men in shabby overcoats standing apologetically by piles of junk or down-and-outs holding individual items in their hands, hoping that some good samaritan will offer a few pence for a broken watch or a rusty bicycle pedal. Thirty years ago the scene was much the same: 'Nowhere else in East London have I seen mental poverty so blindingly proclaimed ... bodies and minds that lack all inner cleanliness and outer sanitation. I hope that the dying out of the older men and the civilizing of the rest may lead to its disappearance before long.' So wrote Robert Sinclair in 1950. Cheshire Street's dustbin market remains – cracked cups, frayed shoes, filthy torn clothes, greasy spectacle frames with broken glass and neolithic electric-light switches.

Westwards along Cheshire Street the traders and their goods become less decrepit. Here one can find incredible bargains for carpets, tools, lavatory bowls, televisions, records, shoes and ex-army clothing. Brick Lane itself has fresh fruit and vegetables, and stalls selling tinned food, buckled cans of peaches or tomatoes with no labels, always popular for storing away for summer holidays or domestic emergencies. From Brick Lane the market once spread along Sclater Street and Cygnet Street to Club Row pet market, officially suppressed by Tower Hamlets Council in 1982 and now redeveloped.

Everywhere there is the excited patter of salesmen, crockery-sellers shouting out lower and lower prices for whole tea-sets, entrancing their audience by throwing plates into the air and catching them. Prices often depend on what the dealer thinks he can get from you, but be on your guard for defective goods. I once bought a perfectly good-looking lump of Cheddar cheese very cheaply here; at home it tasted foul. There is no recourse; even if you found your man next week he'd deny he'd ever seen you.

Chilton Street, parallel to Brick Lane, is known for its bicycles, new and old. The bargains go very early, as soon as dawn is breaking. No doubt most of the bikes are stolen, but the market rights allow the acquisition of stolen goods during daylight hours.

The crowds of Brick Lane attract all kinds of hangers-on – political activists and agitators such as the National Front, religious sectarians, con-men, tipsters and tricksters. There are eccentrics, like the old Russian Jew in the 1950s, known as the silent man, who played ancient 78s which were so worn they made no noise. He collected £500 for settling Jewish refugees in Israel, but died before he got there himself. Descriptions of Brick Lane market in the thirties and fifties all remarked on the drabness of the crowds; except for an occasional group of chattering girls the vast grey sea of loafing people were all men. Today it is more colourful and cosmopolitan.

South of the railway the Spitalfields area has become a Bangladeshi ghetto, with its associated rag trade. The Jews and Huguenot weavers have gone; the smell of curry is everywhere. The buildings in Brick Lane have scarcely changed since the old brick fields were built on in the eighteenth and nineteenth centuries. Neglect and decay abound. An exception is the magnificent Truman's brewery, cleaned and cleverly extended in glass which reflects the courtyard fig tree, iron railings and Georgian façades.

During the week there is a ghastly quiet about the place. A few shops are open, like Blackman's shoe shop in Cheshire Street. A couple of hungry dogs and a white-haired tramp pick their way through a mound of rubbish. The market streets wait uneasily for next Sunday's invasion.

Brixton, SW 9

Merchandise: Very large and varied market, with strong West Indian flavour; good for fresh fruit, vegetables, wet fish and meat, clothes and textiles.

Opening times: 8.30 a.m. to 5.30 p.m. Monday to Saturday. Half-day closing Wednesday.

Location: Electric Avenue, Atlantic Road, Brixton Station Road, Market Row, Electric Lane.

Nearest tube: Brixton (Victoria).

Buses: Nos. 2, 3, 35, 37, 50, 95, 109, 133, 159.

Brixton market is quite possibly the best reason for living in south London. Although it is not as big as the Sunday markets of Petticoat Lane, East Street or Brick Lane, as a daily market it has no rival for size, variety or quality of produce. Brixton is famous for its West Indian community and the market reflects the full gamut of Caribbean life; it sprawls through the streets and arcades either side of the elevated railway, invigorating and stimulating. Even the street names, Electric and Atlantic Roads, are exciting.

The oldest part of the market is Electric Avenue, built in 1890 in ornate late Victorian style with glass-covered verandahs and brilliant electric lighting. The splendour of the street has faded with the years; risk of large vehicles colliding, and general decay, have caused sections of the canopy to be taken down. The Council's ambitiously expensive renovation plans had to be tailored, but the pavements are now colourfully paved and the whole environment is smarter and better cared for than five years ago. As the street curves round to Atlantic

Road it is lined with traditional barrows and stalls selling fresh food and household necessities.

The market extended into Brixton Station Road in the 1920s. Enclosed shopping arcades were formed in Electric Lane and Market Row, between Atlantic Road and Coldharbour Lane. In the thirties Brixton market was noted for its fresh food, but otherwise was drab, with serious-minded housewives plodding silently round the stalls and costers producing scant cheer.

Over the last twenty years the atmosphere and character have changed; the West Indians have brought the market to life. Today people stop to chat and laugh, Bob Marley's music pounds out of the record stall beside Atlantic Road, and the women barter for their food. Everywhere stalls are laden with yams, green bananas, coconuts, plantains, sweet potatoes, cho-cho, and uglis. Bright pink pigs' tails, cows' feet, and strange yellow sides of beef are piled on the butchers' slabs. Grocers sell tinned ackee (a great Jamaican delicacy), cassava flour, egusi, herbs, kola nuts, soursubs and patties. Best of all are the fish: red mullet, shark, pollock, sprats, chub, salted coley, cuttle and goat fish. The Caribbean Sea is full of weird and wonderful fish and most of them can be bought at Brixton, but you probably need to be West Indian to know what to do with them. There must be at least a dozen fresh fishmongers in the market, the biggest concentra-

Electric Avenue, Edwardian splendour, 1907
(Lambeth Archives Library)

tion in London. Jeffries at No. 5 Market Row has been at Brixton for forty years and has changed with the times.

Including the arcades with their permanent kiosks and shops there are over 300 stalls in the market. Flypitching is a problem on Saturdays, cheap crooks here today and gone tomorrow, out to make a quick buck, annoying the regular stall-holders and ratepayers. The market buzzes with activity, colour and gaiety. In the aftermath of the notorious riots and the Scarman Report, Brixton market is the most reassuring place to witness people of all shades living together and enjoying it. No Londoner should miss it.

Broadway Market, E8

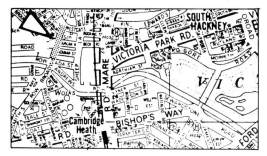

Merchandise: Mainly food.

Opening times: 9.30 a.m. to 4 p.m. Friday and Saturday.

Location: Broadway Market, north of Regent's Row.

Nearest railway station: Cambridge Heath (Liverpool Street).

Buses: Nos. 6, 35, 55, 106, 253 (Mare Street), no. 236 (Westgate Street).

Broadway Market presents a microcosm of Hackney: it is very mixed. The street looks a lot better than five years ago. Brick façades have been cleaned, vast amounts of Urban Programme money have been spent, but half the shops and pitches are empty. Broadway Market was a 1960s clearance area; massive modern blocks replaced the little terraced houses and ambitious plans were made for a new shopping precinct. What was once a thriving market serving a strong local community degenerated into a depressing collection of decaying properties. Now regeneration is in vogue, but it's almost too late. At best, on a sunny Saturday, twenty stalls are sprinkled along the street. The road closure halfway down provides a focus for a few hardened traders.

The curving street still has character and potential. The cobbles survive, though irritatingly disrupted by gas-board tarmac. Many old buildings remain, some improved, some derelict. The fascia of Geo. Tallett's fish shop can faintly be deciphered above the corrugated iron, seemingly condemned for demolition. Beside London Fields the Cat and Mutton pub has been smartened, and Selby's art gallery is perhaps a portent. The Market House

Tavern is painted cheery red, and near the canal estate agents' boards herald bijou residences.

There's still much to be done. Rate-capping may prohibit further public help. Original stone-carved street names indicate former side streets long gone. Has too much been lost? Will yuppie newcomers in studio flats really want to buy all their daily needs from Broadway Market? Perhaps in five years time we shall be pleasantly surprised. Broadway Market community workers insist optimistically that things are improving. Graffiti which once adorned a flank wall – 'Broadway Market is not a sinking ship, it's a submarine' – has been removed; however, Broadway Market has not yet quite floated back to the surface. New shoppers and more activities will help to restore buoyancy.

Catford Broadway, SE6

Merchandise: Fresh food, clothes, household goods.

Opening times: 9 a.m. to 5.30 p.m. Saturday. A few stalls daily.

Location: Catford Broadway between Rushey Green and Catford Road, and Winslade Way.

Nearest railway station: Catford (London Bridge, Victoria).

Buses: Nos. 1, 36, 47, 54, 75, 141, 160, 185.

Street trading in Catford began in the 1880s in the busy thoroughfare of Rushey Green. In 1929 Lewisham Borough Council moved the stalls into Springfield Park Crescent and, rather inappropriately, renamed this narrow street Catford Broadway. In the 1930s it attracted about fifty stalls on Fridays and Saturdays selling a mixture of food, clothes, crockery and carpets. One side of the street was demolished for the new Town Hall, designed like those at Walthamstow, Hackney and Islington in the fashionable Bauhaus style, with shades of fascist grandeur. The market fizzled out after the war and in the 1950s a new shopping arcade, Winslade Way, was built parallel to Catford Broadway.

The Council revived the market in the Broadway in 1976, licensing thirty-five pitches for Saturdays only, since when it seems to be doing well. It is a quiet street, on one side the white sterile hulk of the municipal offices, the other a crescent of small shops surmounted by unusual gothic windows set in tiny gables. The market stalls and the shops sell nothing surprising, although Black's, the camping specialists, have a shop. One fruit stall on the corner of Winslade Way operates all week, and inside the precinct in front of Tesco is a cluster of eight daily stalls – fruit, flowers, vegetables, eggs, biscuits, pet food and, best of all, Mr Baptist's fish barrow. Winslade Way is not an inspiring environment but the Catford Ram, a Young's tied house, is always popular. The elaborate wooden façade is a brave attempt to disguise a concrete box.

Chapel Market, N1

Merchandise: Fruit and vegetables on weekdays, general household goods and food at weekends.

Opening times: 9 a.m. to 3.30 p.m. Tuesday, Wednesday, Friday and Saturday; 9 a.m. to 12.30 p.m. Thursday and Sunday.

Location: Chapel Market, between Liverpool Road and Penton Street.

Nearest tube: Angel (Northern).

Buses: Nos. 4, 19, 30, 38, 43, 73, 153, 171, 196, 214.

Chapel Market is one of the joys of living or working in Islington. While Islington has seen more than a normal share of social change the market remains one of the most genuine and unspoilt of London's street markets.

The seventy or so stalls on weekdays (except Mondays) offer an excellent range and quality of fruit and veg. at very low prices. During the week the market is concentrated at the Liverpool Road end, but on Saturdays and Sundays the whole street fills with stalls right up to Penton Street, and spills over into the side streets. Clothes, crockery, household goods of all descriptions are on sale, as well as food. Many of the shops which line the street also open on Sunday and close on Monday.

Chapel Street was built in 1790 at the same time as St James's Church near by in Pentonville Road. For many years it was a residential street. One of the earliest residents was Charles Lamb's sister, Mary. On leaving Christ's Hospital School aged fifteen, Charles Lamb lived with his sister at No. 44 Chapel Street and worked as a clerk for the South Sea Trading Company in the City. Islington was then still a village, detached from London; Lamb would have walked across fields to get to work. Samuel Taylor Coleridge, a school friend, also lived with the Lambs for a year.

Within fifty years the fields were built on. The householders of Chapel Street had protested when the tunnel for the new Regent's Canal was dug immediately below their homes in 1820. In 1868 another resident complained to the local parish vestry about a butcher's stall which was operating in the street. To no effect; within a few years Chapel Street was an officially designated street market. One of the first Sainsbury's shops opened in Chapel

Chapel Market, 1895, looking west. Note Sainsbury's on the left (Finsbury Library)

Street. The family of Kid Lewis, the middle-weight champ, used to have a linen stall in the market.

Today the market crowds are a cross-section of Islington's mixed society; old ladies with thick stockinged legs which have shuffled up and down this street for fifty years, sensible young mothers in denim dungarees towing prams full of well-fed children, office workers from the Angel and King's Cross, serious social workers and giggling schoolkids. The camembert set from Barnsbury shop religiously in Chapel Market, and why not, when there is also a Marks and Spencer devoted to food and a big new Sainsbury's facing Liverpool Road with a car park to leave the Volvo.

Islington Council has for forty years had its plans for changing the Angel. After years of indecision, huge office blocks are now rising around the junction, mainly for bank headquarters, a new tube station is being built, and the Royal Agricultural Hall with its magnificent Victorian ironwork has become the Design Centre for exhibitions. More shops are proposed in Parkfield Street.

On the east side of Islington High Street, Camden Passage's antique market, shops and expensive restaurants attract tourists and the well-to-do. Islington pubs have been swamped by the real-ale fashion – most welcome, but I hope people actually drink the stuff. Try the Lord Wolsey in White Lion Street for Sam Smith's. As for Chapel Market, while people continue to buy their spuds and avocadoes it won't change. The street cries are still geared to the old ladies: ''Ere yer arr, mum; luverly banar-nars, none of yer rubbish, mum.' Thank goodness for that.

Detergents in sherry bottles, 1968 (G.L.C.)

Chatsworth Road, E5

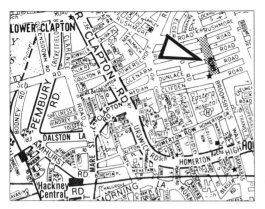

Merchandise: Food, clothes, household goods.

Opening times: 9 a.m. to 4 p.m. Monday to Saturday.

Location: Chatsworth Road, between Clifden Road and Rushmore Road.

Nearest railway station: Hackney Downs (Liverpool Street).

Buses: Nos. 22, 22A (Clifden Road), nos. 38, 55, 106, 253, S2 (Lower Clapton Road).

Chatsworth Road is an unassuming and unremarkable north-east London street, running north from Homerton High Street to Lea Bridge Road. The market consists of about sixty or seventy stalls lining both sides of the road at the crest of the gentle hill which rises above the Hackney Marshes to the east. The parade of small shops caters for everyday requirements and the market stalls sell a similar range of general commodities: vegetables, cheap cosmetics, kitchenware, ladies' clothes, shoes, records and cassettes, toys, sweets and houseplants.

Even when the market is busiest on Wednesdays and Saturdays the pavements are never very crowded. The locals go quietly about their business, a mingling of all colours, brown, black, yellow and white. The stallholders are friendly and have time to chat with their neighbours and regular customers. On a fine morning the sun shines straight down the road, bathing the pavements in warmth and highlighting the three-storey buildings. When it is wet it looks like a very plain street. Apart from the traffic Chatsworth Road hasn't changed a great deal since it was built in 1870.

Choumert Road, SE15

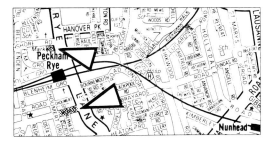

Merchandise: Mostly fruit and vegetables.

Opening times: 9 a.m. to 4.30 p.m. Monday to Saturday.

Location: Choumert Road between Rye Lane and Choumert Grove.

Nearest railway station: Peckham Rye (London Bridge, Holborn Viaduct).

Buses: Nos. 12, 36, 37, 63, 70, 78, 171.

Choumert Road market is tucked away in a side street off the busy Rye Lane. There are about thirty stalls outside the shops along the north side of the street. As is often the case in smaller markets, some of the stalls are run by the shopkeepers. The barrows and the open shopfronts produce an integral display through which the pedestrian has to walk. The shops themselves are small and friendly, including half a dozen butchers. Several specialize in Caribbean and Asian produce, like Amy's West Indian Foods at No. 30.

In 1930 Choumert Road market was much the same, small and good value. However, it was overshadowed by a much larger and better-known street market in Rye Lane which in 1931 moved into a new covered arcade. Mary Benedetta remarked in her charming if somewhat naïve book, *Street Markets of London*, 'It is said this will eventually become the fate of all street markets.' She need not have worried. The white elephant at Columbia market had shown that most costermongers prefer the lower street rents as passers-by can compare prices and wares without obligation.

Choumert Road survived. The indoor Rye Lane market, north of the railway station, was bombed in the war and rebuilt. Now called the Bargain Centre

it is much like any other shopping mall with about a hundred shops selling all manner of groceries, provisions and durables. Rye Lane is a major shopping centre for south London with many large chain stores. The last of the old-style Sainsbury's, with brown marble, tiles and counter service, was at Nos. 61-63, alas now closed. Mixed in are small specialist shops and several individual fruit stalls on street corners. Choumert Road is at the periphery. Like the Choumert Café, most of the local pubs are down-to-earth; the Beehive in Meeting House Lane, north of Peckham High Street, is excellent but a long walk.

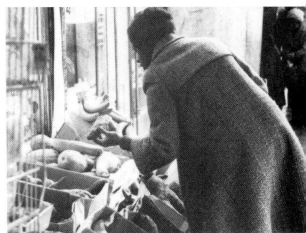

Chrisp Street, E14

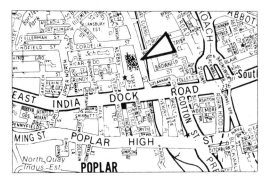

Merchandise: General food, hardware, clothing.

Opening times: 9.30 a.m. to 2.30 p.m. Monday to Saturday.

Location: Market Square, between East India Dock Road and Chrisp Street, Poplar.

Nearest railway station: All Saints (Docklands Light Railway).

Buses: Nos. 5, 15, 40, 106, 277.

This is no longer a market worth a special journey to visit. Just north of the East India Dock Road, the market is now in the middle of the massive post-war Lansbury housing estate, surrounded by huge high-rise blocks. After the devastation of the war the formation of a market square was a deliberate town-planning attempt to create a pedestrian setting for the old market. It has ample room for lots of stalls, including a row of permanent kiosks in an arcade in the middle. It looks prosperous enough and well frequented, with a moderate range of goods on sale, but nothing fancy.

Poplar was once a small hamlet on the country lane which ran across the top of the Isle of Dogs, then a barren marsh. The first primitive dock was built at Blackwall in Stuart times. The Poplar docks were developed by the East India Company in the eighteenth century. For two hundred years the influence of the sea was strong in Poplar, with tall ships' masts and funnels rising over the walls of the docks, the streets thronging with sailors, Chinamen and whores.

A hundred years ago Chrisp Street was a thriving street market, with Jewish sweet-sellers, gipsy love-birds, blind bootlace-sellers and the white rabbit woman. It survived in the 1930s as a genuine local market, less squalid than the frantic touting and Jewish oratory of Petticoat Lane, free of strangers from other parts of London. The bombs and Festival of Britain ethos finished it. The sensible, spacious and well-lit estate pubs, the Festival Arms and the Festive Briton, don't look so admirable thirty years on. Like the utilitarian blocks all around it, the market square with its ugly tower is a dull and functional place. Nellie Walton who died at her stall in 1975 was one of the last pre-war traders. Amid the baked beans and bin liners the gipsy love-birds seem a distant memory.

(Above) Old Chrisp Street, 1890 (Tower Hamlets Library) (Below) 1950, the post-war dream; today looks tattier (G.L.C.)

Church Street, NW8 and W2

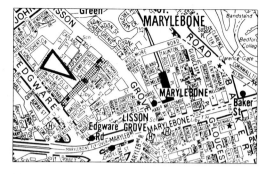

Merchandise: General household and food produce, antiques, bric-à-brac and furniture.

Opening times: 9 a.m. to 5 p.m. Tuesday to Saturday.

Location: Entire length of Church Street from Edgware Road to Lisson Grove.

Nearest tube: Edgware Road (District, Metropolitan, Bakerloo).

Buses: Nos. 6, 8, 16, 46 (Edgware Road), no. 159 (Lisson Grove).

Church Street is a market of two distinct halves which together provide the perfect balance between everyday necessities and irregular luxuries. The architecture in the street reflects the different character of the two parts of the market. From Edgware Road to Salisbury Street both sides of the street have been rebuilt over the last thirty years with modern shops and high blocks of flats set obliquely to the road. At this end rows of fruit and veg. stalls compete vigorously for custom and the pavements are choked with shoppers. Dogs and children scurry among the stalls which sell groceries, jeans, handbags, cheap jewellery, lurid artificial flowers, apple fritters and plastic dolls. The balloon man does a roaring trade. Customers are a motley bunch – Hooray Henrys from Little Venice and Maida Vale, Irish housewives from Kilburn, West Indians from Kensal Green, nurses from St Mary's,

Paddington, and dossers who've tottered along from the station.

From Salisbury Street eastwards to Lisson Grove the 'other' Church Street is lined with pleasant nineteenth-century buildings and is a well-known emporium for bric-à-brac and antiques. In the last five years it has moved up-market and become more pricey. Several expensive antique furniture shops, such as Just Desks, now complement the market and near Lisson Grove is Alfie's Antiques, an enclosed arcade specializing in small trinkets and objets d'art. One stall sells white plaster models of Greek gods and the busts of Beethoven which elderly piano teachers often have on their mantelpieces. On Saturday everything is frantic, chaotic and fun.

With over 200 stalls. Church Street is undoubtedly thriving, and traffic is rightly banned on Saturday. The market is a descendant of the Portman market, which was established in 1830 on the north side of Church Street to take advantage of the new railway goods yard at Lisson Grove. Previously Church Street had linked directly with Regent's Park. The railway tracks severed Lisson Grove from the fashionable paradise of the park and after 1830 the Lisson Grove area deteriorated into a slum. The Portman railway market dealt in meat, fruit and vegetables for which, by 1833, it was rivalling Covent Garden. It didn't last. Attempts to inject new life failed. The impressive Marylebone Station and Hotel opened in 1900 and was accompanied by ambitious plans to modernize the

market, involving new buildings centred round a domed hall. Instead, in 1906 the market site was sold, and Church Street itself took over as the market for the locality.

The Theatre Royal, Marylebone, had also been built in 1830 on the south side of Church Street. In the 1890s it was a famous music hall, billing all the stars of the day, but had become a cinema before being bombed in 1941. The Tuscan façade survived until 1962, sadly concealed behind corrugated iron. A new pub, the Lord High Admiral, stands on the site. For refreshment the Regent Snack Bar in Edgware Road is pure 1930s, chromium chairs and peach melba. The Sea Shell in Lisson Grove is one of London's most popular fish and chip shops, serving real mushy peas, but beware the queues. The Victoria Bar in Marylebone Station offers more sumptuous surroundings and good beer.

Douglas Way, SE8

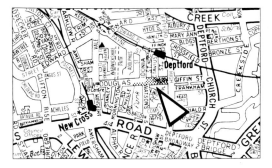

Merchandise: Fruit, vegetables and flowers, hardware, second-hand clothes and junk.

Opening times: 8.30 a.m. to 5 p.m. Friday and Saturday.

Location: Douglas Way, from Deptford High Street to Idonia Street.

Nearest railway station: Deptford (London Bridge), New Cross (East London line).

Buses: Nos. 1, 47, 53, 108, 188.

Douglas Way market lies in the middle of Deptford, one of the more dilapidated parts of south London. Always a poor neighbour of Greenwich, equally old as a riverside settlement, it never attracted the court, fashionable gentry or naval elite. Only Thomas Archer's beautiful St Paul's Church, built in 1730 with its elegant spire, competes with Greenwich.

In the nineteenth century Deptford was full of workers' mean terraced cottages and the riverside cluttered with wharves and warehouses. In 1872 a market for foreign cattle was established to prevent the spread of disease from livestock imported by continental steamship. Each year 150,000 cattle and 200,000 sheep were sold and slaughtered here, mostly for Smithfield. By 1883 street markets existed in Deptford High Street, Deptford Broadway and Edward Street, but in 1921, as traffic congestion mounted, the stalls moved into Douglas Way, a quiet side road off the High Street.

Although Deptford has become depressingly rundown, the market has survived. About twenty-five stalls (fifty on Saturdays) sell fruit and veg., cheese, meat, plants, crockery, toys, haberdashery and clothes. One stall specializes in West Indian vegetables at very cheap prices. Douglas Way is also a good place to pick up second-hand and vintage records. West of Idonia Street, rag-and-bone men and tinker gipsies spread out their bundles of old clothes and junk, and pile it back on to decrepit vans at the end of the day.

Douglas Way is unpretentious and unfashionable. Customers and stallholders are locals, although the dearth of food shops in Greenwich attracts some enlightened people to the market. Now new housing flanks the street, including the Albany Centre where workshops, community rooms and advice services will be an asset to the market. Its jolly design, roof trusses exposed at the eaves, brightens the drabness.

Deptford High Street is a hotch-potch, the genuinely old but crumbling mixed with tidy but bland post-war infill. Several shops cater for the large West Indian community – Laurie's African Food stall by the station and shop at No. 86, Roots Afro cosmetics and groceries at No. 107. Purdie's and Global fisheries sell traditional and exotic fish.

Some of the older and more jaded Deptfordians resent the newcomers, hankering for pre-war days. In reality the immigrants could revitalize the High Street and the market as they have done in Brixton, so long as they get a fair deal. Deptford's future cannot be more bleak than its immediate past.

East Street, SE17

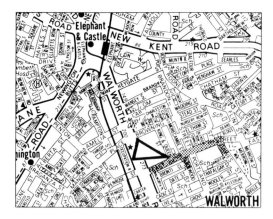

Merchandise: Large choice of fresh food, clothes, toiletries, hardware, household and luxury goods.

Opening times: 8 a.m. to 5 p.m. Tuesday, Wednesday, Friday and Saturday; 8 a.m. to 2 p.m. Sunday and Thursday.

Location: East Street from Walworth Road to Orb Street. Also Dawes Street, Blackwood Street and Deans Buildings on Sunday.

Nearest tube: Elephant and Castle (Northern, Bakerloo).

Buses: Nos. 12, 35, 40, 45, 68, 171, 176, 184.

East Street does not stay awake much after nine on Friday night. There is still Saturday night to come, when everyone goes crazy and nobody goes to bed before eleven. I left while the market was still vividly awake. It would have been a sad sight to see it packing up. Instead I went away with the cries ringing in my ears, the children screaming and playing, and the rain still sparkling under the lamplight in the cracks between the cobbles. (Mary Benedetta, *Street Markets of London*.)

That was sixty years ago when Walworth was one of the poorest areas of south London. On Friday night women bought the supper with the husband's newly won wages; last week's money had run out.

Walworth used to be a marshy area, dissected by tidal creeks, given over to common and rough grazing. It was crossed by East Lane which linked Walworth Road with the Old Dover Road. In the 1770s the common was encroached by squatters and by the mid nineteenth century all trace of rural life had disappeared. The Walworth slums covered every available square yard.

The market began in Walworth Road, probably from the hawking of suburban market-garden produce. When the tram tracks were laid in 1871 a long struggle ensued to move the market. Eventually in 1880 the costermongers were confined to East Lane. At the same time the vestry of St Mary's, Newington, attempted to stamp out Sunday trading and 'clear the evil off the streets'. For a time trading was stopped after 10.30 a.m. on Sunday. Until 1927 the market was a chaotic affair. Each morning when the policeman blew his whistle there was a frantic race for the best pitches in the Lane. It attracted all manner of street entertainers and eccentrics, like Lord Poofum, who in the 1890s sold African herbal snuff endowed with strange powers. Cardsharpers prospered until fingerprinting was introduced. The market was the main amusement for local children including the young Charlie Chaplin.

Today East Street rivals Brixton as the largest south London market. During the week it is busiest on Tuesday, Thursday and Saturday with about 200 stalls, when most shoppers are locals. Sunday is quite different: the expanded market draws people from Croydon, Bexley, Woolwich and Streatham, south London's answer to Petticoat and Brick Lane. Unlike Petticoat Lane, East Street market has enormous variety. There is a regulation that there should be at least four stalls between any two of the same trade. The whole street is therefore a great mixture: bananas, Brylcreem, balloons, bras, books and brushes. There is an eight-year waiting list for stalls; pitches are closely guarded and kept in the family. Immigrants can't get a look in; inevitably there are lots of suitcase flypitchers.

Most of the stallholders are locals to the marrow. Elsie Tomkins's family has sold flowers in Walworth for a hundred years. As a nipper her husband sold bunches of lavender door to door; her mother, unable to afford a market pitch, pushed a barrow through the streets selling mint. East Street breeds characters. 'Old Bob' Smith, ex-bare-fist prize fighter, pioneered street trading in bananas in the 1880s and was given a huge coster's funeral in 1926. The Fox family, the cap kings of East Street since 1920, now sell only about fifty caps a year, so they have diversified into general clothes.

East Street has its specialities. On Sundays Blackwood Street is a plant and flower market. A few stalls sell 'cabbages' – cheap clothes made out of left-overs (see Roman Road). There is the sarsaparilla man dispensing iced pineapple juice. For more intoxicating refreshment try the George IV, Masons Arms or Royal Albert in East Street, or the Crown near by in Brandon Street. One special tradition from the old slum days survives – East Street market is always open on Christmas Day.

Hammersmith, W6

Merchandise: Mainly fresh food and flowers.

Opening times: 9 a.m. to 5 p.m. Monday to Saturday. Half-day closing Thursday.

Location: South end of Hammersmith Grove between King Street and Beadon Road.

Nearest tube: Hammersmith (Metropolitan, Piccadilly, District).

Buses: Nos. 9, 11, 27, 33, 72, 73, 220, 283, 295 (Hammersmith Broadway).

After a decade of being hounded from one temporary site to another by redevelopment schemes, Hammersmith market has at last a permanent home. The twenty stalls are now huddled together on the east side of Hammersmith Grove, right in the heart of the King Street shopping centre. Mercifully the market lies away from the choking exhaust fumes and the rushing traffic which make Hammersmith Broadway a nightmare.

No one really knows when Hammersmith market began. In the nineteenth century the market was in King Street near the Hop Poles Inn which is a stone's throw from the present market. When interviewed in 1884 one of the costers reckoned the market had been there for a hundred years; he himself had been there for forty. King Street became a tramway in 1883, but it took twenty-three years of prolonged legal action before the barrowmen were moved into Bradmore Lane. Some obstinate ones were imprisoned. The market stayed in Bradmore Lane until 1972 when the land was required for redevelopment. Bradmore Lane was engulfed in a huge new complex of department stores, multi-storey car parks, offices and the new Lyric Theatre. The market was moved into Beadon Road and amid protests was shovelled from one empty site to another until 1978, when Hammersmith Grove was chosen.

The market has a friendly family atmosphere which contrasts with the hygienic sterility of the new King's Mall shopping precinct. Most stalls sell food: Bill Rochford, now over seventy, has sold fruit for sixty years; brother Alf runs a flower stall; and there are two fish barrows, Tydeman's, and Rann's which has shrimps, whelks and mussels. Prices are not especially cheap but the quality is reliable, attracting discerning customers from Barnes, Chiswick and Kensington. The wholefood stall, with nuts, honey, muesli and lentils, is popular. Unusually for a street market, it is active on a Monday, the old-fashioned wash day. A suggestion for Sunday trading was opposed by the stallholders who said they needed the rest!

The King's Mall has everything you would expect to find – Mothercare, Habitat and posh shoe shops. Just round the corner from the market in Beadon Road are three splendid surprises: Turner's florists, Sellar Bros. architectural ironmongers, and The Big Cheese, a delicatessen with goats' cheese, baguettes and home-made pâté. If you're fed up with shopping and can face crossing the Great West Road, take a stroll beside the river where the scullers skim by, the air is fresh and the riverside pub, the Dove, offers its time-honoured hospitality.

Hampstead Community Market, NW3

Merchandise: Fresh food, clothes, jewellery, hardware.

Opening times: 9.30 a.m. to 6 p.m. Saturday.

Location: Next to the old village hall at No. 78 Hampstead High Street.

Nearest tube: Hampstead (Northern).

Buses: Nos. 46, 268.

The Hampstead Community Market opened on 19 September 1975 on the Blue Star Garage site on the east side of the High Street just below Flask Walk. The Hampstead Community Trust played a big part in establishing the market and ensuring a wide variety of goods among the sixty stalls. Antiques and bric-à-brac could have flooded the market – there were over 400 applications – but the Trust provided a list of the basic trades they wanted to see and directly controlled twenty of the stalls.

From the first day the market was a success; a tempting array of stalls with colourful canopies provided by the operators, set at the focal point of the High Street. When the Blue Star site came up for development the market moved to the other side of the road into the alley and yard next to the old village hall, now the Community Centre. The range of goods on sale has been maintained – fresh fruit and vegetables, a butcher, dairy produce, tinned food, adult and children's clothes, pottery, haberdashery, jewellery and hot snacks. One of the best permanent stalls is Foster's Fish Shop which sells every sort of fresh and smoked fish you can think of. Inside the Community Centre there is more of a W.I. village fête flavour to the stalls.

Hampstead, which I once heard described some-what misguidedly as London's Montmartre, is always an entertaining place to walk around. On weekends you have to pick your way through the astrakhan coats and dressed-up strollers trailing their Afghan hounds. The Americans love it. There are some wonderful and expensive shops, like the Rosslyn Delicatessen at No. 56 Rosslyn Hill which has the most amazing selection of cheese and charcuterie, all perfection. If you have a sweet tooth you won't be able to resist the Louis Patisserie in Heath Street, a short stroll down Perrins Lane. There are plenty of plush places to eat, but Pippin's Vegetarian Restaurant almost next door to the market is good value.

Too many Hampstead pubs are overcrowded, unfriendly or affected. My favourites are the Well Tavern, slightly off the beaten track in Well Walk, or the public bar of the Flask in Flask Walk, full of beer-swilling trombonists and old boys playing dominoes.

Hildreth Street, SW12

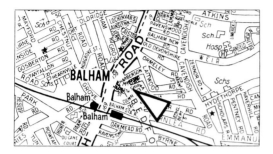

Merchandise: Food, flowers, haberdashery, household goods.

Opening times: 9.30 a.m. to 5 p.m. Monday to Saturday. Half-day closing Thursday.

Location: Hildreth Street, between Balham High Road and Bedford Hill.

Nearest tube: Balham (Northern).

Buses: Nos. 88, 131, 155.

Balham, gateway to the south, is the beginning of true suburbia. The Hildreth Street market is something of a surprise, a cosy collection of thirty stalls in a short traffic-free street. Like most of the rest of Balham, Hildreth Street was built in the 1880s. The shopping streets are three-storey red-brick gables, surrounded by an amorphous sea of neat terraced houses. It could be Muswell Hill, Harlesden, Chiswick or Streatham. Bedford Hill is

older, originally a private drive to the house of the Duke of Bedford and the Priory, another large aristocratic mansion. Priory House, built in 1830 in Strawberry Hill gothic, still survives up the hill.

Late Victorian Balham consisted of respectable middle-class, homely houses for City clerks and factory managers, free from the smoke and squalor of Battersea, Lambeth or Southwark. A market began in Bedford Hill in about 1900 but soon moved into Hildreth Street when the electric trams arrived in 1903. In the 1920s an indoor market opened in Bedford Hill opposite Hildreth Street. Today it struggles on as the Balham Continental Market, enclosed in a now rather dilapidated building; Hildreth Street has more life and a good selection of stalls. The High Road has all the big shops but Balhamites like Hildreth Street for its fruit and veg., cheap soap and pot plants. Most of the barrows are engraved 'Lambeth Walk'; Hildreth Street offers a more stable home.

Most of Balham's pubs are vast, rambling and Edwardian. The Duke of Devonshire, a short way north in Balham High Road, is a typical south London Young's house, with lots of different bars, ordinary people and good beer. On Friday nights the lads are out with their birds and Ford Cortinas, and the old codgers moan in anticipation about tomorrow's match at Crystal Palace.

Bedford Hill, 1902, before the trams arrived (Wandsworth Library)

Hoxton Street, N1

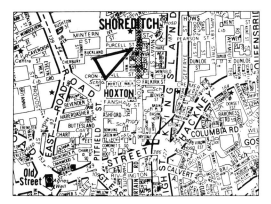

Merchandise: Mainly food.

Opening times: 9 a.m. to 5 p.m. Monday to Saturday.

Location: Hoxton Street, south of Nuttall Street.

Nearest tube: Old Street (Northern).

Buses: Nos. 22, 48, 67, 149, 243 (Kingsland Road).

Moving east from the affluence and gentility of Camden and Islington, Hoxton is where the East End begins, its most westerly outpost. Beyond Hoxton lies the huge area of Bethnal Green, Bow, Old Ford and, further out, Stratford, West Ham and Ilford, a segment of London unknown and unvisited by many. Hoxton Street market, once the main street of the medieval hamlet of Hoxton, has a sad drabness today. There are spaces marked out in the roadway for over 200 stalls, but in mid-week only about twenty are occupied: fruit and vegetables, a flower girl, a wet fish stall and a couple of barrows loaded with junk. Saturday is better, but still a shadow of the pre-war market when people from all over Shoreditch and Finsbury flocked to Hoxton Street where hundreds of barrows were crammed into the street and crowds of children clustered round the sweet and toy stalls.

It is hard to imagine that in Tudor times Hoxton was a jolly place, known for its entertainments and rural pursuits. A certain Ben Pimlico, landlord of one of the more rumbustious taverns, gave his name to Pimlico Fields, which were used for archery, and

Pimlico Walk off Hoxton Street, where Ben Jonson fought a duel.

Hoxton was a popular residence for actors and comedians. Shakespeare acted here in a small barn converted into a theatre and Hoxton church was London's actors' church until Covent Garden was built up. The theatrical tradition in Hoxton survived and flourished in the nineteenth century.

Hoxton market in Shakespeare's day was a small affair selling country produce to village folk. Engulfed in the spread of bricks and mortar in the eighteenth and nineteenth centuries, rural Hoxton was transformed into the most overcrowded part of Shoreditch. In 1820 the market outgrew the old market square at the south end of the village and moved first into Pitfield Street and, in 1840, into Hoxton Street where it sprawled for its half-mile length. Together with Bethnal Green, Hoxton was the criminal headquarters of London, a receiving centre for robberies carried out all over the City. Violence was common on the streets; the Hoxton

Market Gang were notorious for their thuggery and racketeering.

Charles Booth's survey of East London in 1889 showed the highest concentration of extreme poverty in Hoxton. This continued into the 1920s, the vicious traditions ensuring that social workers and East End charities avoided Hoxton. Slum clearance, wartime destruction and the northward spread of business from the City have emptied Hoxton. Such was its ghastly reputation that many people evacuated during the war either had no home to return to or preferred to settle elsewhere.

Hoxton today is a social tomb. The old marketplace just off Pitfield Street is a desolate site, with rows of empty parking meters. A few Georgian houses survive in Hoxton Square, but it is a no-man's-land caught between the opulent City and residential Hackney. One day something will happen; at the moment there is an eerie ceasefire.

The Geffrye Museum in Kingsland Road is well worth a visit. In 1715 Sir Robert Geffrye, an ironmonger and Lord Mayor, built the beautifully proportioned almshouses which now house a fine display of domestic English furniture from Tudor to modern times, and old shopfronts. The Royal Standard (Young's) opposite is convenient and, though modern, not unpleasant. The pubs in Hoxton High Street are less inviting. The famous Britannia Theatre in Hoxton Street was bombed and demolished soon afterwards. Now, halfway up the street on the east side, Hoxton Hall breathes new life. This old music hall is now restored as a community centre and community theatre. The hall itself with its balconies and high stage is small, intimate and marvellous for kids. Terry Goodfellow who runs the show is a man of conviction and vision. Hoxton Hall is a ray of hope. At last people are beginning to go to Hoxton again.

Inverness Street, NW1

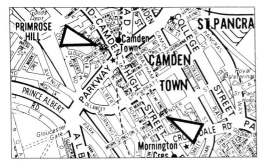

Merchandise: Mainly fruit, vegetables and junk.

Opening times: 9 a.m. to 5 p.m. Monday to Saturday. Half-day closing Thursday.

Location: Inverness Street, off Camden High Street on the left going up.

Nearest tube: Camden Town (Northern).

Buses: Nos. 24, 27, 29, 31, 68, 74, 134, 135, 168, 214.

Inverness Street is one of north London's liveliest markets. Its popularity was illustrated a few years back when 4,000 people signed a petition against the Council's action to reduce the number of stalls of one trader.

The street was built in 1860; the market probably began at about that time in Camden High Street but was gradually forced into side streets when the traffic became too bad. Some of the stalls went into King Street, renamed Plender Street in 1946 after a local magnate, which is further down the High Street. Only five licensed stalls survive there now, and Plender Street market, like the old markets at Goodge Street, Earlham Street and Parker Street, has dwindled away.

Inverness Street has fifty pitches and lots of old regulars. John Pheney has had forty years in the fruit business, while Reg Stone, subject of the petition, followed his father into the rag-and-bone trade. Reg has sold pots, pans and prams at the market for thirty years. There is an excellent cheese stall with a good range of English and Continental cheeses at below delicatessen prices. There are cut-price pet foods and a lovely cut-flower stall. Custom is so good that in 1979 the traders applied for a Sunday licence; it was refused on grounds of noise.

Haral's Greek Food Centre at No. 12 Inverness Street has been going for thirty years. They sell a wide variety of European and Oriental foods, not just Greek, such as beans, pulses, nuts, olives, pasta, herbs, spices and sausages. Camden High Street has a large range of shops, from Talby's fishmongers to Tesco. The nearest decent pint is Young's at the Spread Eagle in Parkway.

Jubilee Market and Earlham Street, WC2

Old Covent Garden Market, 1850 (G.L.C.)

Merchandise: Clothes, crafts, novelties, household goods, foods. Second-hand books (Earlham Street).

Opening times: Jubilee and Apple Markets – 9 a.m. to 5 p.m. daily. Earlham Street – 10 a.m. to 4 p.m. Monday to Friday.

Location: Jubilee Market on south side of Piazza next to Southampton Street; Apple Market within renovated market; Earlham Street off Shaftesbury Avenue.

Nearest tube: Covent Garden (Piccadilly).

Buses: Nos. 1, 6, 9, 11, 13, 15, 77, 170, 176, 196 (Strand), nos. 14, 19, 22, 24, 29, 38 (Cambridge Circus).

Old Covent Garden has changed beyond recognition. Where the gutters were once choked with crushed cabbage leaves, the pavements stacked high with boxes of oranges and the bollards biffed by lorries, there is now neatness and gentility. The restoration of Fowler's market buildings is very fine but the character has gone, the gruff oaths of porters and the unique mixture of bananas and ballerinas.

For a while after the fruit and veg. moved to Nine Elms in 1974, Jubilee Market provided some continuity with the earthiness of the old days. Threatened with demolition, the market had a spontaneous tattiness. Now the Jubilee Sports Hall has been saved and slickly re-styled, and the shed on the corner with Southampton Street redeveloped with a high block of luxury offices and apartments. The market beneath now matches the smart self-consciousness of the whole area, attracting lunch-time browsers and tourists. The food stalls fulfil a purpose; the others – selling ornamental candles, ethnic bangles, joss sticks, paper butterflies, vintage 78s, Edwardian dolls and silverware – duplicate the expensive shops which abound in Covent Garden.

The Apple Market within the northern section of Fowler's buildings is tasteful but equally artificial. Here dozens of stalls sell Bohemian clothes, jewellery and trinkets, while tourists pose for their photos. Nothing offends but nothing excites. The buskers at the other end are auditioned to maintain standards and usually draw crowds; so do the jugglers, mime artists and acrobats on the cobbled forecourt of St Paul's. This is grockle-land par excellence, no place for market bargain-hunters.

For several years Camden Council have tried to revive the much older Earlham Street market. In the last century this market (known then as Little Earl Street) prospered in the heart of the Seven Dials slums. Until recently it was a tawdry selection of reject shoes and back-edition girlie mags. Now

half a dozen second-hand book-sellers have settled here, including prints and manuscripts, in keeping with the theatreland and literary character of Charing Cross Road and St Martin's Lane. At No. 14 the lovely hardware shop of F. W. Collins is a rare relic of old London.

Elsewhere the gentrification process marches on irrevocably and few empty sites or derelict properties remain untouched. Rocketing rents force out old-timers. Happily there are still good reasons to visit the district – the Monmouth Street Coffee House, Paxman's french-horn makers and Stamford's map shop in Long Acre, or Penhaligon's perfumery at No. 41 Wellington Street, with its beautiful old shopfront and exquisite apothecary

atmosphere inside. Neal's Yard wholefood shop, one of Covent Garden's trend-setting pioneers, has moved to plusher premises in Short's Gardens and is no longer the cheapest place in town. The water clock amuses onlookers and drenches the unwary.

Covent Garden seems to be *the* place to go in the evenings and at weekends. Many shops have to stay open late as part of their lease. The Opera House, newly extended, and the Transport Museum draw their own crowds. There are dozens of places to wine and dine, and lots of packed pubs. The Marquess of Anglesey, convenient for the Opera, and the Lamb and Flag with its dark stained woodwork and low ceilings tucked away off Garrick Street, are old favourites.

Lambeth Walk, SE11

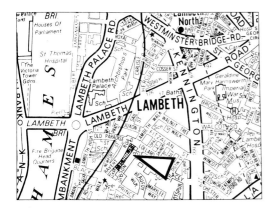

Merchandise: Fruit and vegetables, clothes, haberdashery, household goods and toiletries.

Opening times: 9 a.m. to 5 p.m. Monday to Saturday (busy only Friday and Saturday).

Location: Lambeth Walk shopping precinct, between Black Prince Road and Old Paradise Street.

Nearest tube: Lambeth North (Bakerloo).

Buses: Nos. 3, 10, 44, 159 (Lambeth Road).

'Any time you're Lambeth way, any evening, any day, you'll find us all doin' the Lambeth Walk.'

So sang Lupino Lane in 1937 in the first performance of Noel Gay's *Me and My Girl* at the Victoria Palace. A myth was born of pearly kings and queens sitting on winkleshell thrones, scoffing bowls of jellied eels washed down with foaming tankards of stout, exchanging free-and-easy banter in quaint cockney rhyming slang.

The glamorous stage image was based on the Lambeth Walk street market in the heart of the Lambeth slums, in reality a long narrow street built in 1830 lined with dingy two- and three-storey shops and houses which on Friday and Saturday nights came alive with all the fun of the fair. Like the Victorian markets at Whitechapel, the Brill, East Street and Hoxton, Lambeth Walk was more than carrots and cabbages. Friday was pay day for labourers and servants and a time for revelry. There were organ-grinders, Gainsborough hats, quacks selling panaceas, apple fritters, hot chestnuts, fag-

gots and pease pudding, acrobats and strongmen, shooting galleries, hokey-pokey men, ginger beer vendors, luridly coloured sweets and greasy oil lamps, jostling crowds and hundreds of strident voices. The pubs roared with song and laughter.

The war brought it all to an end. Bombs knocked the stuffing out of the area and in the 1960s the

Lambeth Walk in 1946 (Lambeth Archives Library)

Awaiting demolition, the mews behind Lambeth Walk, once used by French onion-sellers (Lambeth Archives Library)

G.L.C. embarked on the comprehensive demolition and redevelopment of what was left. Lupino Lane never saw the final demise of Lambeth Walk; he died in 1959 and was buried next to pianist Charlie Kunz in Streatham. The companionable terraces were replaced with corrugated iron, seas of concrete and mountains of bricks. The market dwindled. In 1972 Queeny Bock, one of the ten remaining stallholders, retired after fifty years selling lingerie; she and her cat, who purred contentedly among the lace, knew everyone. Robert and Daisy Bateley soldiered on behind their vegetable stall until they were the only stall left.

In 1976 the new pedestrian Lambeth Walk shopping precinct was opened. Gordon Ley who had helped serve on his grandfather's stall took a greengrocer's shop and, as secretary of the traders' association, initiated a summer street festival with bunting and amusements to revive the market. Initial enthusiasm faded. By 1979 two stalls were left and Lambeth's Health and Consumer Services Committee decided to launch a last-ditch campaign to save the market. Stallholders' rents were reduced

from £6.50 to £1 for Friday and Saturday. Low rents seemed to do the trick; by August 1980 there were thirty stalls. Now, despite the danger of overfast expansion, at least the market is worth going to. The Bateleys are still there, after over fifty years in Lambeth Walk.

The golden days are gone. The Jolly Cockney and the Lambeth Walk pubs are reminders of the past, when the market stretched from Black Prince Road to China Walk, when Marcantonio's ice cream, Harvey and Thompson pawnbrokers and Burrough's Eel and Pie shop flourished and the French onion-sellers kept their bicycles in the back mews behind Paradise Street. Millions of feet once sauntered, shuffled, stomped or stumbled along Lambeth Walk. Even before the market existed Lambeth Walk, known then as Three Coney Walk, attracted visitors to its mineral water wells and archery butts. The modern precinct is a grim, alien place, town planning at its most brutal. The market could bring it to life and revive the old legends. For that to happen people must start going there again, to do the Lambeth Walk.

Leadenhall, EC3

Merchandise: Game, poultry, fish and meat.

Opening times: 7 a.m. to 4 p.m. Monday to Friday.

Location: Whittington Avenue, off Gracechurch Street and Leadenhall Street.

Nearest tube: Bank (Central, Northern), Monument (Circle).

Buses: Nos. 15, 25 (Leadenhall Street), nos. 35, 47, 48 (Gracechurch Street), nos. 10, 40, 44 (Fenchurch Street).

Set in the heart of the City of London, close to the Stock Exchange and Nat West tower, Leadenhall market is a delightful enclave of tradition. As a retail market its history outspans any other; the superb freshness and quality of the food on sale mark it apart from any other market in London.

'Ledenhalle' in 1296 was the manor house of Sir Hugh Neville, and was noted for its great lead-clad roof. Forty years later the house was damaged by fire and the land acquired by the City authorities who established a poultry market on the site. In 1345 new regulations ordered all poulterers who were not freemen of the City to sell their birds at Leadenhall. This favoured London traders who operated at the east end of Cheapside, known to this day as Poultry. Leadenhall was thus reserved for country people selling country produce.

By Tudor times Leadenhall had evolved into a more general provisions market. In 1598 Stow described Leadenhall: 'sometime inhabited by poulterers, but now by grocers and haberdashers'. When the market was rebuilt after the Great Fire, the enclosed space was divided into three: the beef market, Green Yard with general shops, and the herb market, with fishmongers and poultry. Next to the poultry section stood the Beehive Tavern from which Beehive Passage takes its name.

The New Moon at the other end of the market is reputedly the Blue Boar where Sam Weller hung out. Dickens was obviously familiar with the market: Tim Linkinwater in *Nicholas Nickleby* boasted that he could buy new-laid eggs in Leadenhall any morning before breakfast, and so pooh-poohed the idea of life in the country having any advantage over the City!

In 1881 the old buildings were replaced by a grand new arcade designed by Sir Horace Jones, architect to the City Corporation. The new Leadenhall was spacious and airy like Jones's earlier designs at Smithfield and Billingsgate. The fine cast-ironwork is painted cream and maroon and proud stone arches guard each entrance to the market. There is a central crossing of the four avenues, surmounted by a cupola.

For a hundred years Leadenhall has operated as a market specializing in game, fish, poultry and high-quality provisions. It is tailored to an upper-class clientele, and priced accordingly. Traditions and old customs survive: salmon, rainbow trout, oysters, crab and lobster are sold off the open marble slab at Ashdown's; Ashby's make their own sausages; grouse, mallard, quail and guinea fowl are sold in season by Butcher and Edmonds, and you will find hare, venison and wild boar if you want it. Many dealers also supply wholesale, hence the early morning start, presumably to livery company banquets. Bespectacled men sit behind mahogany desks taking telephone orders.

Sadly the tradition of live poultry before Christmas when City workers could inspect their goose or turkey 'on the hoof' has died out. Today there are a great range of shops: fruiterers, delicatessens, snack bars, all catering for the lunchtime shopper. The market pubs, like the Lamb selling Young's ales at the centre of the market, the New Moon and the Bunch of Grapes, are packed at lunch with pin-stripes. They, like the market, are closed at weekends, when the weekday hubbub is replaced by a ghostly world of pecking pigeons and scurrying cats, until another Monday.

(Following page below) Christmas week, 1953, a turkey hanging from every hook (G.L.C.)

Leather Lane, EC1

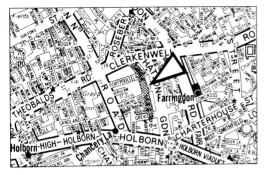

Merchandise: Food, clothes, household goods.

Opening times: 10.30 a.m. to 2 p.m. Monday to Friday.

Location: Leather Lane, between Clerkenwell Road and Greville Street.

Nearest tube: Chancery Lane (Central), Farringdon (Circle, Metropolitan).

Buses: Nos. 5, 55, 243 (Clerkenwell Road), nos. 8, 17, 22, 25 (Holborn), nos. 18, 45, 46, 171A (Gray's Inn Road).

Gently curving south to north from High Holborn to Clerkenwell Road between Gray's Inn and Hatton Garden, Leather Lane is an ancient street. In medieval times it was a small farm track running northwards along the high ground of the west bank of the River Fleet, known then as Stoke Lane or in contemporary Flemish 'Le Vrun Lane'. By the time of Stow's *Survey of London* this had been corrupted into Lither Lane, 'a turning to the fields, late replenished with houses'. A street market was soon established as the area developed in the seventeenth century into a slum district. 'The Lane traverses a very poor neighbourhood, infested with thieves and beggars, and is in itself narrow and dirty, lined with stalls and barrows and itinerant dealers in fish, bacon, vegetables and old clothes.' Just off Leather Lane, near Holborn, Brooke's market became established as a small but popular open-air butchers' market.

During the nineteenth century Leather Lane remained a prosperous working-class market, thriving on Friday and Saturday nights when newly won

weekly wages were spent. The new dead meat market, which opened at nearby Smithfield in 1868, ruined Brooke's market. A small paved square with benches and trees remains, together with the name. It is better known today for Thomas Chatterton, the poet, who lived and died at No. 38.

By the 1930s Leather Lane was quieter, selling fruit and veg., thoroughly safe and respectable. Fifty years on it is one of London's busiest lunchtime markets. The growth of offices in Holborn in the fifties and sixties has ensured a large high-earning clientele, while between Leather Lane and Gray's Inn Road the retention and rehabilitation of Peabody estates has kept the local population. The mix of locals and office workers is good for the character of the market.

There are about 150 licensed stalls, and at least 100 in action most days of the week. The range of goods is enormous – lots of clothes, handbags, toiletries, tinned groceries, electrical goods, and even a nice bicycle spares stall. The whole street has a pleasant feel, except at the southern end where the redevelopment of the former Gamages site has introduced building on a massive scale, alien to the small market stalls in Leather Lane.

Most of the buildings are Victorian shops and houses. On the left side as you walk up is a lovely pawnbroker's shop, still operating, with the three giant golden balls hanging above the pavement. This is just one reminder of the proximity of the Hatton Garden trade, with its Jews and jewellers. If the bustle makes you thirsty, the Clock House further up on the right is a crowded but merry pub with solid hot food and a good pint of Bass or I.P.A.

Lewisham High Street, SE13

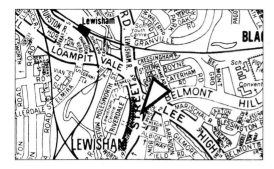

Merchandise: Mainly fruit and vegetables; also flowers, fish and haberdashery. Separate crafts market.

Opening times: 9 a.m. to 5.30 p.m. Monday to Saturday; craft market 8.30 a.m. to 4.30 p.m. Monday.

Location: West side of Lewisham High Street, south of the Clock Tower. Craft market in Riverdale Hall, Rennell Street, off the High Street.

Nearest railway station: Lewisham (London Bridge).

Buses: Nos. 1, 21, 36, 47, 54, 89, 108, 122, 178, 180, 181, 185, 208, 261.

The aftermath of the bomb, 1944. The clock tower survived the blast (Lewisham Library)

The market in Lewisham High Street has suffered more adversity than most. At 9.44 a.m. on 28 July 1944 a VI rocket, undetected by radar, landed 100 yards south of the clock tower on the busy market in the middle of Lewisham shopping centre. The blast killed fifty-six people, seriously injured a further ninety-nine and completely demolished a 500-foot frontage in the High Street. The air raid warning sounded at 9.46 a.m. Despite the loss of a generation of traders the market had recovered by 1947 to fifty-five licensed stalls. Since then most of the west side of the High Street has been re-developed for a new covered shopping precinct. On the pavement the street traders have carried on undeterred.

Back in the 1900s the High Street market was one of south London's liveliest. Stalls stayed open until eight at night, midnight on Saturday, the barrows lit feebly by spluttering naphtha flares. It was full of characters like Mrs Hilliard who sold celery and wore heavy gold earrings and a feather in her cap. German bands tortured the ear with their chords, drowning the hurdy-gurdy players and Italian ice cream Johnnies, complete with melodeon and monkey. Itinerant pedlars sold matches, collar studs ('two a penny'), bootlaces, pins and needles – mostly beggars hoping for charity.

Lewisham market was known for its horse dealers – Hoppy Thew, named after his club foot, Levi Boswell, a handsome gipsy with black curly hair, and Jack Rags. Jack bought his horses at Barnet Fair, and was commonly regarded as a half-wit, perpetually ridiculed and abused. Few understood his miraculous gift for training and quietening wild or frightened horses.

In 1919 Lewisham Council moved the market stalls into a side street and allocated pitches to ex-servicemen. By the early thirties unlicensed traders were operating again in the High Street and in 1934 a long struggle ensued to evict them. The protestors won the day and the High Street became the official marketplace.

Forty out of the sixty stalls today sell fruit and veg., traditional and good quality: R. and F. Davis, presumably brothers, at the south end are reliable

for good wet and shellfish. The rest are mainly clothes. Paxton's haberdashery stall is excellent, festooned with an immense selection of ribbons, reels of cotton thread, buttons and hooks. The Riverdale shopping centre is like most big shopping malls of the seventies – predictable shops, hot air and piped 'musak'. Lewisham has all the major stores, even C. & A.; shoppers come from far and wide, which is good for the market. On Mondays a small craft fair has started in the Riverdale Hall off Rennell Street – some thirty stallholders peddling old postcards, glass, china, prints, clocks, copper and brass paraphernalia. It's not in the same league as Camden Passage, but interesting nevertheless, especially on a day of the week when most of London's markets are traditionally quiet.

Lower Marsh and The Cut, SE1

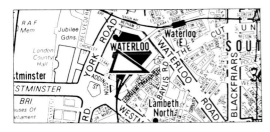

Merchandise: Household goods, clothing, fruit and vegetables.

Opening times: 10.30 a.m. to 2.30 p.m. Monday to Saturday.

Location: Lower Marsh, from Westminster Bridge Road to Baylis Road.

Nearest tube: Waterloo (Northern, Bakerloo).

Buses: Nos. 1, 4, 5, 68, 70, 76, 149, 168, 171, 176, 177, 188 (Waterloo), nos. 12, 53, 77, 109, 170, 184, 196 (Westminster Bridge Road).

The street market in Lower Marsh has a long and varied history. Once much bigger and known as the New Cut it rivalled the Brill in Somers Town as one of the largest and roughest working-class Victorian street markets. Today it is a smaller affair, confined almost entirely to Lower Marsh and busy only during weekday lunchtimes.

As the name suggests, Lower Marsh was low lying and liable to flooding. Lambeth Marsh, in a bend of the River Thames, was used as pleasure grounds and remained undeveloped until, in 1786, a road was cut from Westminster to Blackfriars Bridge – the New Cut. Over the next fifty years the land was protected from flooding by the embankment and covered by obnoxious industries, cheap housing and the great railway station named after Napoleon's last stand.

The Lambeth Parish Vestry minutes indicate that by 1845 a street market in the New Cut was arousing complaints because of obstruction and religious outrage at Sunday trading. A costers' petition seeking formal permission for their stalls was refused in 1856; they simply carried on regardless. In any event the Vestry were more concerned with nuisance from fat-melting, blood-boiling and piggeries.

The New Cut market on Saturday and Sunday was an extraordinary scene of squalor and hilarity. The shops were of the cheapest kind and, for the benefit of the very poor, rows of costers' barrows sold fruit, old clothes, rat traps, villainous-looking sweets, cats' meat and artificial flowers. After dark evil-smelling naphtha lamps flared and crowds of women in black shawls surrounded the butchers

The New Cut, 1896. The Windmill pub is in the middle distance (Lambeth Archives Library)

who auctioned their unsold perishables; they called it 'being at the murder'. Children scoured the gutters for fallen fruit or dragged wooden boxes home for firewood.

New Cut was an unsavoury place; the police kept in pairs. Even in 1936 Mary Benedetta 'did not linger in New Cut, but fled away home'. She was shocked by the deathly pale faces of the women, eyes staring out of hollow cheeks, coated with grime like coalminers. The poverty contrasted with the luxurious comfort of Waterloo's pullman trains, evoking visions of transatlantic liners or the Orient Express.

New Cut and Great Charlotte Street were renamed The Cut in 1936, and after the war the market contracted into Lower Marsh. Now there are just one or two vegetable stalls left on the south side of The Cut opposite the Windmill pub. The market today relies heavily on lunchtime office workers from County Hall and the Shell Centre; few tourists are attracted over the river from Parliament Square. A hundred stalls sell the usual range of greengroceries, cheap fashionware, cut-price cosmetics and lavatory brushes. The varied shops are mainly small and friendly. Some of the old favourites have gone, like Thos. Porter who smoked fish in his own backyard, but the street remains pleasantly seedy considering its location. For the thirsty the two pubs, the Artichoke and the Spanish Patriot, offer unpretentious refreshment.

John Sainsbury started work as a grocer's assistant in New Cut before opening his own shop in Drury Lane in 1869. By 1914 there were 115 branches, but the headquarters remained in Waterloo in Stamford Street. The Royal Victoria Theatre, now the 'Old Vic', was built on the corner of Waterloo Bridge Road and the New Cut in 1818. Lilian Baylis made it London's most famous music hall. After years of neglect it has been renovated and re-opened. Waterloo has its old faithfuls; actor Tommy Godfrey, who as a boy used to pull his father's barrow from Covent Garden before school, has always lived in The Cut. The triumph of homes over offices in the Coin Street battle has given the community a shot in the arm, but Waterloo now apprehensively awaits the impact of the Chunnel terminal.

Northcote Road and Clapham Junction, SW11

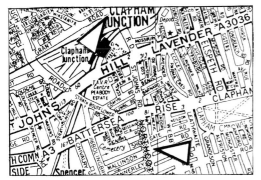

Merchandise: Northcote Road – mainly fruit and vegetables. Junction market – clothes and hardware.

Opening times: Northcote Road – 9 a.m. to 5 p.m. Monday to Saturday. Junction market – 9 a.m. to 5 p.m. Friday and Saturday.

Location: West side of Northcote Road from Battersea Rise to Bennerley Road. Falcon Road north of railway bridge.

Nearest railway station: Clapham Junction (Victoria, Waterloo).

Buses: No. 49 (Northcote Road), nos. 19, 37, 77, 249 (Battersea Rise), nos. 39, 45 (St John's Hill), nos. 35, 156 (Falcon Road).

Northcote Road is typically south London – late Victorian terraces in dull grey brick and small local shops, with quiet residential side streets, neat homes for the respectable lower middle classes. The southern part of the old parish of Battersea was not developed until the 1870s. A shopping centre grew up close to the huge railway junction at Clapham which in turn attracted street traders. By the 1890s there were costermongers in Falcon Road, Lavender Hill, St John's Road and Northcote Road, much to the annoyance of many shopkeepers who disliked the competition. The Ratepayers' and Tradesmen's Association repeatedly lobbied for their removal. In 1910 the costers were evicted from their pitches in St John's Road, and Northcote Road became firmly established as the local street market. A few clumps of stalls continued in Lavender Hill until the thirties.

Northcote Road has forty-five stalls on the busiest days, Friday and Saturday, nearly all selling fruit and veg. It is still primarily a market for locals but, being the only large food street market for some distance, it attracts shoppers from Wimbledon, Wandsworth, Clapham and even Chelsea. St John's Road contains the large non-food High Street chain stores which complement the market.

Northcote Road is doing well. The increase in numbers and prosperity of customers has encouraged stallholders to sell more exotic and varied produce – aubergines, pimentos and kiwi fruit – as well as the English basics. The proximity of New Covent Garden wholesale market at Nine Elms has been good for the stallholders who used to buy at Borough or old Covent Garden.

Some of the shops have also become more adventurous. Acquired Taste at 9 Battersea Rise has an excellent choice of cheeses, pâtés and herbs. An equally pleasant contrast is Dove and Son, the best butchers in the area, who have been in Northcote Road since 1889.

The street traders have had their share of worry from threats of increased charges. The costs of street cleaning, rubbish disposal and health inspection are met from stallholders' rents, not from the rates. Higher charges mean less competitive prices on the stalls, fewer customers, declining numbers of barrows, and rising charges for those who are left to foot the bill. Already many barrows are run by older men; youngsters are less willing to work the long hours in all weathers.

Clapham Junction market is newer and precariously established, shunted from one empty plot to another, at present on the grubby corner of Falcon Road and Grant Road, through the gloomy bridge. The previous large St John's Hill site has gone for posh shops and flats. A dozen stoical stallholders sell clothes, cheap toys and packaged foods, and hope for better days. In the background trains rumble through the Junction. This is the land of the Ladykillers and the Lavender Hill Mob and, of course, the Clapham omnibus. If the wind is right you can whiff the Young's brewery at Wandsworth. The Plough in St John's Hill serves the end product.

North End Road, SW6

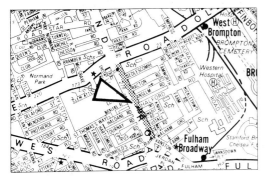

Merchandise: Large range of fresh food, groceries, flowers, hardware and luxuries.

Opening times: 9 a.m. to 5 p.m. Monday to Saturday. Half-day closing Thursday.

Location: East side of North End Road, south of Lillie Road to Vanston Place.

Nearest tube: Fulham Broadway (District).

Buses: Nos. 28, 30, 74, 91 (Lillie Road), nos. 11, 14, 295 (Fulham Broadway).

North End Road market is probably about a hundred years old. Jerdan Place beside Fulham Broadway was known until 1877 as Market Place, and was presumably the market for Walham Green. The market began to spread up North End Road in the 1880s, augmented by costermongers who had been booted off their pitches in King's Road by shopkeepers. Booth noted in 1902 that the King's Road shopkeepers were rueing their action, for North End Road flourished, attracting trade from miles around. At its peak in the 1920s the market stretched from Fulham Broadway right up to Hammersmith. New regulations for street markets in 1927 enabled the local council to restrict the market to south of Lillie Road.

In the thirties Fulham was entirely working class, with no hint of the middle-class invasion which came forty years later. The market was noted for its cheap food, variety of produce and quick service. Mary Benedetta had 'yet to find a shop that comes up to it in this way'. On Saturday evenings costermongers auctioned off their surplus, offering incredible bargains simply to be rid of their stock.

The market has outlived all sorts of ephemeral proposals to move or close it. In 1934 the L.C.C. and Ministry of Transport wanted to turn North End Road into a major arterial road linking the new Wandsworth Bridge with Cromwell Road. As a first step they asked the borough council to remove the stalls to Seagrave Road. The street traders, shopkeepers and Chamber of Commerce fought the plans tooth and nail, which paid off; the ideas were forgotten during the war and have never revived.

Fulham is now fashionable and expensive, providing comfortable, compact houses for designers, solicitors, West End dealers and media men. Amazingly the market has changed very little. Fruit and veg. stalls like Frank Freddie's are still cheap and there is a great selection of goods – flowers, eggs, crockery, toys, jewellery, fabrics and floor polish. The stallholders, like Albert Hersey who has run his fish barrow for twenty-seven years, have done well out of the influx of affluence. There is a long waiting list for licences and few of the ninety pitches are ever empty. North End Road has lots of good shops, not just Sainsbury's and Marks and Spencer but also small traditional shops. Goodall's the butcher at No. 435 and Shell the baker at No. 354 are excellent. Both shopkeeper and stallholder know they are good for each other, which makes North End Road one of London's best food markets. The new Earl's Court market in the Lillie Road car park is excellent for fabrics.

Queen's Crescent, NW5

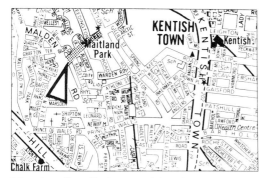

Merchandise: Fruit, vegetables, clothes.

Opening times: 9 a.m. to 1.30 p.m. Thursday.
9 a.m. to 5 p.m. Saturday.

Location: Queen's Crescent, between Malden
Road and Grafton Road.

Nearest tube: Chalk Farm or Kentish Town
(Northern).

Buses: Nos. 24, 46.

This small friendly street market is much valued by
residents of Kentish Town and Belsize Park.
Compared with some larger markets it offers
nothing very special in either price or variety but it
has a nice atmosphere.

The Crescent was built in the 1860s, part of a new
suburban estate called Maitland Park which helped
to fill the gap between Hampstead village and
London. The market began soon after. Between the
wars Kentish Town was solidly working class, an
area of backyard industries and large terraced
houses divided into lodgings, peeling stucco and
grimy brickwork blackened by railway smoke.

In the early 1970s Malden Road was almost
entirely redeveloped on both sides. For several years
Queen's Crescent market was on its knees and
didn't look like getting up. The street became
empty, a few traders carried on quietly beside their
stalls while the bulldozers roared in the background. Fortunately the market survived to see
better days. Now there are large new housing
estates along Malden Road, Mansfield Road and

Grafton Road – pretty hideous, but at least people
live there, and people must eat to live and shop to
eat. The shabby terraces of Kentish Town and
Belsize Park are also shabby no longer. Stripped
wood front doors, colourful roller blinds and freshly
painted front walls are signs of the middle-class
invasion and its fashions. This influx has helped the
market's recovery just as much.

On Thursdays and Saturdays about eighty stalls
set up, with most of the fruit and veg. at the Malden
Road end, clothes, leather goods, toys, cosmetics
and haberdashery towards Grafton Road. The
shops are small and friendly, including a traditional
fish and chip shop with a timber and tiled front.
There is a pub at each end of the market and one in
the middle, the Dreghorn Castle, with a jolly mural
on the street corner opposite.

John Sainsbury opened his second shop – his first
branch store – at No. 159 Queen's Crescent in 1876.
Although it is now occupied by Studio Prints the
original tiled back wall with the Sainsbury motif is
clearly visible through the shop window.

Queen's Market, E13

Merchandise: Fruit, vegetables, fresh meat, fish and eggs, clothes and hardware.

Opening times: 9 a.m. to 5 p.m. Monday to Saturday. Half-day closing Wednesday.

Location: West side of Green Street, next to Queen's Road.

Nearest tube: Upton Park (Metropolitan, District).

Buses: Nos. 58, 162, 238, S1 (Green Street).

Queen's Market will be familiar to any dedicated West Ham supporter, a stone's throw from the claret-and-blue gates and next to Upton Park station. Facing Green Street bold green letters on the canopy announce the market, a large covered square packed with stalls and surrounded by shops. Until quite recently it was open to the skies; the roof was added by Newham Council in 1979.

The medieval parish of West Ham boasted a Tuesday market and an annual fair but both had fizzled out by the eighteenth century. The church suppressed attempts to hold a pleasure fair on Whit Monday at Plaistow in 1806. Not until the 1880s did a small street market spring up in Green Street in response to the thousands of new neat terraced houses. Even this didn't last long; a double line of tram tracks laid in 1904 uprooted the costers. The old Gravel Field in St Mary's Road was suggested but instead the barrowmen chose Queen's Road.

Since moving to the new square when the Green Street frontage was rebuilt in 1969 the market has prospered and expanded. Now there are always over 100 stalls, twice as many on Saturdays. The two fish stalls are noteworthy, one concentrating on the traditional English taste for cod, whiting, skate and haddock, the other supplying exotics like snapper, red mullet, flying fish and squid for the West Indian palate. Among the poultry, eggs, bacon and fresh vegetables are Asian specialists such as Kyber Halal Meat, and dozens of non-food stalls – clothes, cosmetics, crockery and chrysanthemums.

The roof is a great improvement, not quite as elegant as Leadenhall but equally effective. People go about their business quietly and methodically. Talk is of football, the dogs, Mrs Next Door's marriage or poor old Flo's operation, as well as the 'shocking price of spuds'. It is a marketplace and a meeting-place.

Queen's Road market, 1925 (Newham Library)

Rathbone Street, E16

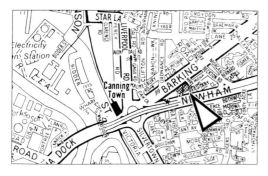

Merchandise: Fresh fruit, vegetables, meat, eggs, fish and poultry, household goods.

Opening times: 9 a.m. to 5 p.m. Tuesday to Saturday. Half-day closing Wednesday.

Location: South side of Barking Road, close to Newham Way flyover.

Nearest railway station: Canning Town (Stratford).

Buses: Nos. 5, 15, 58, 69, 241, 276.

The great East End market tradition continues beyond the Lea Valley. Rathbone Street market is central to life in Canning Town, where the community has somehow survived the upheaval of massive post-war redevelopment. Old Rathbone Street was swept away in the early 1960s together with a thousand slums. A market had begun here when costers were moved from the old Victorian markets in North Woolwich Road, Victoria Dock Road, Barking Road and Freemasons Road. The local board had tried unsuccessfully to close these main-road pitches back in 1886, and in 1904 police helped to shift the truculent traders. By 1911 Rathbone Street was well established and received an extra boost when Victoria Dock Road market finally ceased in 1920.

Since 1963 the market has occupied a spacious triangular site fronting the Barking Road with a backcloth of new shops and housing estates. The 140 pitches, arranged in several lines, sell a fair range of fresh vegetables, meat, poultry, eggs and fish, cut flowers and pot plants, and a typical array of clothes, cheap jewellery, soap, watch straps and cuddly toys. The cat and dog meat stall is special, one of the few left in London. Eager dogs with their owners in tow queue for their unappetizing lumps of flesh and offal while all the neighbourhood strays scamper round sniffing for scraps.

The shops are what you would expect – a Presto supermarket (formerly Caters), cheap shoes and sliced white bread. Behind the shops traffic hurtles along the new flyover and Newham Bypass, smashing a corridor through Canning Town, though Barking Road is more pleasant as a result. Rathbone Street market itself seems jolly and cheerful, and the Royal Oak opposite is nice enough; all the more so when compared with the austerity of the lower Lea Valley, a dreary landscape of strident pylons, angular gantries, curvaceous cooling towers, slumbering gasworks and comfortless waterways.

Ridley Road, E8

Merchandise: Large variety of fresh food and groceries, including West Indian fruit and vegetables, clothes, jewellery and hardware.

Opening times: 9 a.m. to 5 p.m. Tuesday to Saturday.

Location: Ridley Road between Kingsland High Street and St Mark's Rise.

Nearest railway station: Dalston Junction (Broad Street).

Buses: Nos. 22, 30, 38, 48, 67, 76, 149, 243, 277.

Ridley Road is north London's answer to Brixton market. It is at its best on Friday and Saturday. In summer the loud-coloured shirts and dresses of the West Indians, equally loud reggae music and stalls heaped with yams, cassavas and green bananas evoke a calypso atmosphere more like Jamaica than Dalston.

Ridley Road is close to the busy junction of Ball's Pond Road and Dalston Lane and runs beside the North London line, built in 1850 as the East and West India Docks and Birmingham Railway. The land was once owned by Nicholas Ridley, Bishop of London from 1550 to 1553. A small market of about twenty stalls began at the Kingsland Road end of Ridley Road in the 1880s. A fair used to be held on the waste land to the north.

When street trading regulations were introduced in 1927 the new requirement for a three-foot gap between stalls lengthened the market from the tight cluster at one end. By the 1930s Ridley Road was attracting 200 traders on Saturdays. It also lured more unpleasant elements; gang warfare, vendettas and protection rackets were rife in Dalston. More sinister, it was a Fascist breeding ground: Ridley Road was a favourite rendezvous for the anti-

semitic Blackshirts and, after the war, for Oswald Mosley's Union Movement. In 1947 mounted police broke up violent clashes between Fascists and Communists in Ridley Road.

Today a few National Front slogans are chalked on walls but, by and large, Ridley Road market is a cosmopolitan and lively place. The West Indians and Asians, accustomed to street bartering, have given it a great boost. Ridley Road is fun and, with chain stores like Boots and Sainsbury's near by in Kingsland High Street, draws big crowds. An unusual feature of the market – the permanent shacks along the south side of the street which spill out on to the pavement like medieval shops but lock away at the end of the day. The western end of the market sells mainly food, Caribbean and indigenous; further along are clothes, fabrics and trinkets, all with a strong ethnic flavour. One hopes that the ugly scenes of the thirties never return.

Shepherd's Bush, W12

Merchandise: Enormous range of food, household items and luxury goods, with a strong multi-racial flavour.

Opening times: 8.30 a.m. to 6 p.m. Tuesday to Saturday. Half-day closing Thursday.

Location: On the east side of the railway viaduct between Uxbridge Road and Goldhawk Road.

Nearest tube: Shepherd's Bush (Metropolitan, Central), Goldhawk Road (Metropolitan).

Buses: Nos. 12, 207 (Uxbridge Road), nos. 88, 237 (Goldhawk Road), nos. 11, 49, 72, 105, 220, 260, 283, 295 (Shepherd's Bush Green).

Shepherd's Bush, together with Brixton and Ridley Road, is the most cosmopolitan of street markets. On Saturday it is a babble of foreign tongues, like an eastern souk: the fast guttural haggling of Arabs, the jibber-jabber of Indians, the deep-throated bellows of cockneys, the excited chatter of Africans and Jamaicans mingle with the cries of yelling babies, pulsating music from record stalls and trains rumbling by overhead. The market has become popular with the Arabs: for the young sheikh in his immaculate cream robes, his women with their beaky face masks and the servants in their black tunics, Shepherd's Bush market is the nearest thing in London to a kasbah. They must find the formal terraces of Kensington and Bayswater a little strange; Shepherd's Bush is home from home.

The market stretches for a quarter of a mile, gently curving beside the railway viaduct. Each of the forty-six arches has one or two shops or lean-to stalls while the roadway, closed to traffic, is packed with barrows and booths. The variety of things

Laying the sewer beside the railway, 1909 (Hammersmith Library)

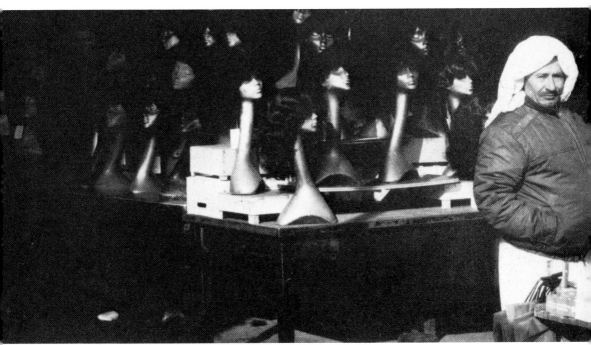

for sale is staggering – gaudy fabrics, Afro wigs, plastic flowers, outsize girdles, bamboo curtains, pet food, football rosettes, patna rice, bangles, saucepans, sandals, carpets, cut-price toiletries, and foam chips for cushions. There are dozens of fruiterers, butchers and grocers, and an excellent fishmonger, W. H. Roe! A high proportion of the stallholders are Asians; many of the customers are West Indians and Africans, patronizing stalls piled with cassava, plantains and cho-cho, and the Caribbean travel agent.

Although the railway was built in 1864, the market started in July 1914 when a Mr John Crowe leased land from the railway company and set up some stalls. After the Great War, during which the railway arches were used for billeting troops and stabling horses, the market started up again, this time with the railway retaining control. Following complaints about the health risk, the roadway (known then as Railway Approach) was drained and paved. In 1930 the market was extended west of the railway on to the old Silver Cinema site fronting Uxbridge Road. The owners, Winner Investments, tried to buy the rest of the market from London Transport in 1961, but failed. The Silver Cinema site was closed and built on in 1969. Since then the market has continued to be run by London Transport, who derive a handsome income from the tenants.

Some of the old market favourites have gone now, such as Uncle Albert's toffee apple stall. The B.B.C. Lime Grove studios still back on to the other side of the arches, but the yashmaks, saris and turbans colour the market. For the culturally sensitive the Railway Arms at the Goldhawk Road end offers traditional restorative medicine.

(*Above left*) Market busker, 1953 (Hammersmith Library)

Southwark Park Road, SE16

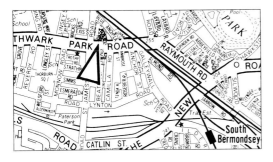

Merchandise: Fruit, vegetables, wet fish, flowers.

Opening times: 9 a.m. to 5.30 p.m. Monday to Saturday.

Location: Market Place, Blue Anchor Lane, beside Southwark Park Road.

Nearest railway station: South Bermondsey (London Bridge).

Buses: Nos. 1, 70, 70A.

'Going down the Blue' is an old Bermondsey custom. The market has always been known locally as the Blue, after Blue Anchor Lane. Before the last war the market was one of the largest in south London – over 250 stalls packed both sides of Southwark Park Road from Yalding Lane to the railway bridge, and people came from far and wide. In the 1950s the council tried to move the market to a new site off the street where it would cause less obstruction to traffic. The costers, reluctant to leave the kerbside and lose the passing trade, opposed the move furiously. Meanwhile the council succeeded in reducing the size of the market by not renewing licences when they expired. The traders struggled on against all the odds.

Eventually in 1976 the market was relocated in a new shopping precinct on the north side of Southwark Park Road just west of old Blue Anchor Lane. After initial doubts and fears of extinction the market seems quite happy in its new position. There is room for about forty stalls: on weekdays there are about a dozen traders, on Saturdays about thirty. The new piazza with its benches and young trees looks quite attractive in the summer. Many of the older stallholders, however, are nostalgic about the pre-war days. Florence Weller, who is one of London's most senior flower-sellers, remembers Christmas times when her father decorated the family stall with artificial flowers and the traders auctioned off their goods late on Christmas Eve. On Friday and Saturday evenings the market was a place where people came for fun and enjoyment, to meet friends and have a good time; Bermondsey folk didn't have television then.

There are two useful fish stalls, Palmers' and Hodges', both families with three generations in the market. Alan Hodges fears that fish is pricing itself out, and that his generation will be the last of the market traders. The market has to compete with a Tesco and a giant Co-op store, and Holden's hardware shop which spreads all over the pavement opposite. One hopes that Hodges' prophecy will not turn out to be correct.

The 'Blue', Southwark Park Road, 1928 (Southwark Library)

Strutton Ground, SW1

Merchandise: Fruit and vegetables, clothes, household goods.

Opening times: 11.30 a.m. to 3 p.m. Monday to Friday.

Location: Strutton Ground, off the south side of Victoria Street.

Nearest tube: St James's Park (Circle, District).

Buses: Nos. 10, 11, 24, 29, 70, 76, 88, C1 (Victoria Street).

Strutton Ground is a short narrow street lined by three-storey properties with shops, just along from the Army and Navy Stores. After the canyon of Victoria Street with its bland glass and concrete blocks and incessant traffic – surely the most American street in London – Strutton Ground market is a welcome refuge for lunchtime shopping. It is not an area where one would expect to find a street market, being so close to some of the more respectable institutions of British life such as Westminster Abbey, the Houses of Parliament, Buckingham Palace, Scotland Yard and the Home Office.

Whether or not peers used to strut up and down this street when they came out of the House of Lords, Strutton Ground is a very old thoroughfare, originally an ancient path which ran beside the Stourton Meadows used by monks and peasants

travelling from the fields and orchards to the abbey at Westminster. South of Strutton Ground, Horseferry Road was a track crossing the marshes to the ferry between Westminster and Lambeth palaces. Until Westminster Bridge was built in 1752 the ferry was the only method of crossing the river with a horse and cart; it didn't close until Lambeth Bridge opened in 1862.

In Tudor times Stourton Meadow was bought by a cousin of Elizabeth I, Lord Dacre, who erected Stourton Houses on the south side of what is now Tothill Street. As the court at Westminster grew, pressure for development mounted. The meadows were drained and the land acquired for building. Strutton Ground and the surrounding streets were laid out in 1672 by Sir Robert Pye, M.P. for Westminster and parliamentarian during the Civil War. Old Pye Street is named after him, and not the piepowder courts (see page 15). Stourton House was demolished in 1718 by which time Westminster was already a fashionable residential area. It remained quite isolated from London, surrounded by market gardens. Artillery Row was used for archery practice; the old butts were not removed until the early 1800s.

The market probably began as a place for buying and selling locally grown vegetables to the well-to-do new inhabitants. It is therefore one of London's older street markets. Victoria Street, driven through by the Victorian road engineers, almost obliterated it; but it survived. Today it thrives on the lunchtime custom of office workers. Prices are not low, but the quality of fruit and vegetables is reliable. The other stalls sell women's clothes and cut-price basic household goods – soap, scouring powder, toothpaste and shoe polish. It is a small version of Leather Lane. At No. 6 is Stiles the baker's whose excellent bread is often hot out of the oven.

If you ignore the monstrous buildings of Marsham and Victoria Streets it is a very pleasant area. St James's Park is a delight in all seasons, and there are also the lunchtime concerts at St John's, Smith Square. Good beer can be found in the Buckingham in Petty France, but don't bank on getting a seat.

Swiss Cottage, NW3

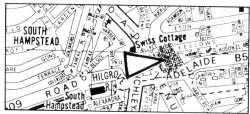

Merchandise: Pot plants, bric-à-brac, food, books and clothes, new and second-hand.

Opening times: 9 a.m. to 5 p.m. Friday, Saturday and Sunday.

Location: The Square, behind Swiss Cottage Library and Baths; also inside the Community Centre on Sunday.

Nearest tube: Swiss Cottage (Jubilee).

Buses: Nos. 13, 31, 46, 82, 113, 268.

After the turmoil and disruption of the 1970s, after years of shifting from one blighted site to another, it has turned out alright in the end. Swiss Cottage market at last has a permanent home. It is the end of an era – the three-pronged battles between local community-minded enthusiasts, the bureaucratic Council and unconcerned property developers are over, here at least. The hoardings have gone, so too the builders' bulldozers and the unorganized market which scattered itself spontaneously over the empty land. Rumours of rats and rabies, complaints of riff-raff and rowdies, and campaigns for babies, bicycles and bottle-banks have receded into the past. Solutions have been found and everyone has grown older.

Red and white 'bakelite'-style offices have now been built on Avenue Road, with luxury flats on Winchester Road. Between the two a buoyant, well-organized market thrives in the newly created square beside the Community Centre, thirty stalls decked in jolly red and white awnings selling an excellent range of goodies – eggs, cheese, fruit and veg., flowers and plants, half-price paperbacks, jewellery and second-hand clothes. It is a pleasant traffic-free place to wander and browse, with a landscaped garden and football pitch as well. Amazingly the Hampstead Theatre and the Citizens' Advice Bureau survived the upheavals too.

The Community Centre, which serves tea and coffee and offers a toddlers' play area, runs the market, which is fortunate. Poor old Camden Council, who never did much for the stallholders, now struggle to keep the library and swimming pools open on their shoe-string budget. So much for their sports hall pipedreams which would have wiped out the market square. At last everybody can get on with living again.

Tachbrook Street, SW1

Merchandise: Fruit, vegetables, flowers, fish.

Opening times: 9.30 a.m. to 4.30 p.m. Monday to Saturday.

Location: North end of Tachbrook Street between Warwick Way and Churton Street.

Nearest tube: Pimlico (Victoria), Victoria (District, Circle).

Buses: Nos. 2, 36, 36A, 185 (Vauxhall Bridge Road), no. 24 (Belgrave Road).

This is Pimlico's market, a small but good market which gets bigger and better on Fridays and Saturdays. Its nucleus is Tachbrook Street by the junction with Warwick Way, spilling into Churton Street when busy. It is a friendly place to shop, free of the bustle and pressure of markets in more commercial areas; there is time for a smile, a quip or a chat. Most of the customers are residents: ex-East Enders rehoused on the prize-winning Lillington Street estate, beautifully designed by Darbourne and Darke in warm red brick; comfortable gentry from the posh squares; Italians and Cypriots from multi-occupied lodgings; or the middle-class trendies from their desirable 'Georgian' (in fact Victorian) terraces. None of the tourists who fill the hotels of Belgrave Road find their way here, but are whisked away by coach to other honey pots.

Pimlico was originally a swamp, flooded by the tidal Thames, good only for oysters and watercress. It was drained in the 1620s for pleasure gardens and named after Pimlico Fields in Hoxton. The white stucco terraces and squares didn't appear until the 1870s. The old marsh had been fed by the Tach Brook, which was a deltaic extension of the Tyburn, flowing from Marble Arch through Green Park, St James's Park (feeding the lake) and south to Victoria. Like London's other lost rivers the Tach Brook is now submerged in sewers and culverts.

The market deals mainly in food: lettuces, aubergines and pomegranates, fresh eggs, shellfish and poultry. On the corner with Warwick Way is Wright's the fishmonger, established over a century ago; Ivano, a Venetian greengrocer, at No. 44 Tachbrook Street is excellent; Gastronomia Italia at No. 8 sells all the salamis, hams, cheeses and pastas the local Italian community could wish for. It is not all food; Cornucopia has all kinds of memorabilia and wonderful thirties cast-offs. For rumbling stomachs Grumbles in Churton Street is a splendid local café, chaotic but charming. For a stand-up cup of coffee try Costa's in Vauxhall Bridge Road and buy some beans while you're there, or sit down at Costa's Café a few doors down for a coffee and croissant.

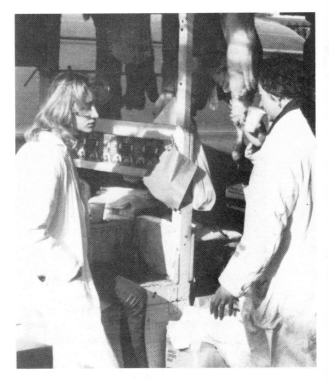

Walthamstow High Street, E17

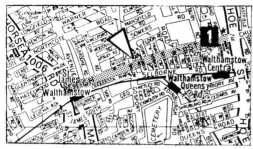

Merchandise: Food, household goods, clothes, DIY, gardening equipment and plants, toiletries, luxury goods.

Opening times: 8 a.m. to 5.30 p.m. Thursday, Friday and Saturday.

Location: Walthamstow High Street, from Hoe Street to Blackhorse Road.

Nearest tube: Walthamstow Central (Victoria).

Buses: Nos. 20, 34, 48, 58, 69, 158, 206, 230, 236, 262, 275.

With its busy bleak main roads and featureless side streets of monotonous two-storey terraces, Walthamstow doesn't superficially hold universal attractions, but the house of William Morris at Lloyd Park and the great High Street market provide ample justification for a special visit. Walthamstow reputedly has the longest street market in Britain, stretching for over half a mile east to west from Hoe Street down to Blackhorse Road with an unbroken line of 500 stalls, and has been drawing crowds from all over north-east London for nearly a century.

It is not a journey to be undertaken lightly; on a Saturday the struggle through the dense throng from one end to the other will take well over an hour, and that's without joining the queues to buy anything! It is not the place to become impatient or battle against the flow; give yourself time to enjoy the jostle and revel in the variety, choice and quality of goods for sale. After the dull similarity of produce on offer in many of London's smaller general markets, Walthamstow is remarkable for its special-ist stalls – fresh-smoked kippers, nuts and dried fruit, gardening tools, wallpaper, key-cutting, Hoover spares, dog meat, toys, make-up, swimming costumes, sunglasses, lead crystal and cut glass engraved on the spot, cheap farm eggs, Wellington boots . . . so it goes on, and on, often with duplicates to compare prices. You may see some of the traders at the Sunday markets at Hackney Stadium or Lea Valley, but many earn enough at Walthamstow.

In the crush of people and welter of merchandise and awnings it is easy to forget the shops behind the stalls, which include a Marks and Spencer and Sainsbury's in the new development on the south side. Sensibly the street has been repaved and all the stalls equipped with plug-in lighting; there are even occasional seats to rest weary feet and arms elongated from the weight of your purchases.

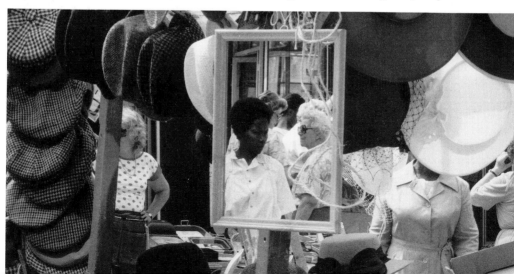

Watney Market, E1

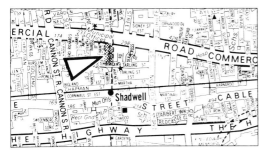

Merchandise: Mainly fruit and vegetables.

Opening times: 9 a.m. to 5 p.m. Monday to Saturday.

Location: Watney Market, off the south side of Commercial Road.

Nearest tube: Shadwell (East London line).

Buses: Nos. 5, 15, 40 (Commercial Road), no. 22A (Cable Street).

plants. George Tobias moved his wet-fish stall from old Watney Street into the new mall. The success of Watney Market is in marked contrast to Lambeth Walk where the new precinct has revived only a shadow of the old market. Perhaps the shops are the reason; Watney Market, like Chapel Market or Ridley Road, has a Sainsbury's which pulls the crowds.

The name 'Watney' may have something to do with the Watney Mann brewery near by in Whitechapel. However, the pleasant pub at the south end of Watney Market, the Thomas Neale, is a free house selling Young's and Sam Smith's. From this elevated position one can look south down the tatty remains of Watney Street. A few shops survive in the small two-storey terraces by the blackened railway bridge. Corrugated iron creaks in the wind, derelict cars lie hopelessly on their axles and rivulets of litter blow along the pavements.

Watney Street used to run between Cable Street and Commercial Road in the heart of the area called Shadwell, near the river and the docks. In the 1820s it was known as Watney Passage until it was widened. A street market began here in the 1850s, and was thriving by 1886, when there were complaints about the obnoxious smell from stalls selling meat and fish. Fish was best value for many poor people. Watney Street was also close to the wholesale fish market opened at Shadwell in 1885 as a rival to Billingsgate. Bitterly opposed by the City Corporation, the new privately owned market was a flop and closed in 1909. The site was converted in 1913 into the King Edward Memorial Park.

Watney Street was badly bombed in the war but the street market carried on into the 1970s. Then the bulldozers moved in to finish the job. The new Watney Estate was built, obliterating the northern half of Watney Street. A new thoroughfare was created, slightly elevated, with shops on either side and tiers of housing behind linked by concrete footbridges. The market was relocated here. Every day there are about twenty stalls mostly selling fruit and veg., with some clothes, toiletries and house-

Well Street, E9

Merchandise: Food and general household goods.

Opening times: 9.30 a.m. to 4 p.m. Monday to Saturday.

Location: Well Street, from Morning Lane to Valentine Road.

Nearest railway station: Hackney Downs (Liverpool Street), Hackney Central (Broad Street).

Buses: Nos. 6, 30, 236 (Wick Road).

Well Street was once part of an old country lane which wandered from Shoreditch to Homerton and the banks of the River Lea. The market dates from the 1850s, ten years or so after the old fields had been covered in little streets of yellow brick houses by the early Victorian speculative builders.

The market occupies the north-east end of Well Street, just off Morning Lane, where the street is narrow and untroubled by through traffic. On the north side the two-storey terraces have round first-floor window arches which peep like eyebrows above the ground-level shopfronts. The market is compact and popular, and on Saturdays about eighty stalls huddle in the street and spill into the side turnings. The produce is predictably like most other small markets in unfashionable working-class areas: dented cans of fruit and battered biscuit packets at reduced prices, fish, haberdashery and polyester shirts; there is an old dear selling incredibly cheap but equally awful greetings cards and wrapping paper. The fruit and veg. is moderately priced but nothing special in quality or variety. The people are friendly and the street has a pleasant cosiness, rather different from the grand but shabby terraces in nearby Cassland Road with their magnificently ornate pediments; it is a refuge from the thundering traffic at Hackney Wick.

Well Street market's greatest claim to fame is that here in 1919 Jack Cohen (later Sir John Cohen, founder of Tesco) began trading from a stall. Despite his humble beginnings and what some might call a degrading job, he was a natural salesman, acutely aware of working-class mentality and motivation. His rapport with the shoppers earned him grudging admiration from older market men. To begin with he sold N.A.A.F.I. surplus – groceries, soap, anything that was going. His secret was rapid turnover, cutting prices to the bone and selling three times as much as the next man. Before long Cohen had stalls at Hoxton, Chatsworth Road, Hammersmith and Caledonian markets; an empire was born. The big new Tesco supermarket in Well Street is a living monument to this self-made man, and a welcome complement to the market.

Whitechapel and Mile End Waste, E1

Merchandise: Whitechapel – fruit, flowers and a great variety of other goods. Mile End – mainly household goods and clothes.

Opening times: Whitechapel – 8.30 a.m. to 5.30 p.m. Monday to Saturday. Half-day closing Thursday. Mile End – 8.30 a.m. to 5.30 p.m. Saturday only.

Location: North side of Whitechapel Road between Vallance Road and Brady Street. North side of Mile End Road from Cambridge Heath Road to Eaglet Place.

Nearest tube: Whitechapel (Metropolitan and District).

Buses: Nos. 10, 25, 253 (Whitechapel Road).

Whitechapel has a long history of markets extending through to the present day. Whitechapel lies just outside the eastern gateway to the City. From Aldgate itself Whitechapel High Street leads out, eventually, to the great farmlands of Essex. The long-established importance of this route explains the enormous width of both Whitechapel Road and Mile End Road. This is nothing to do with the designs of post-war traffic engineers. Centuries of cattle-droving and the great Whitechapel Hay Market ensured that the seventeenth- and eighteenth-century buildings were set as far back as possible from the mud and dung spattered by bullocks' hooves and horse-drawn carts.

Whitechapel, established by Act of Parliament in 1708, was one of the three big London hay markets, the others being Smithfield and Haymarket itself. London's appetite for hay and straw was colossal. The horse was the main form of transport for pulling cabs, omnibuses, traders' vans, private carriages, and for use by the military, the police, and riding schools. The hay markets were the modern equivalent of petroleum depots, except that hay and straw were bulkier than petrol.

Haywains and trams, Whitechapel Road, 1914 (G.L.C.)

Every Tuesday, Thursday and Saturday huge hay wagons rolled in from Essex, Suffolk and Hertfordshire. Some came by barge from Kent and, towards the end, by railway and even lorry! From 7 a.m. to 3 p.m. Whitechapel High Road and the side streets were clogged by carts, big shire horses, red-faced countrymen and the sweet smell of hay. Despite the combustion engine and mounting criticism of the chronic congestion, the market survived well into the twentieth century. Whitechapel was still the largest hay market in the country when the ancient market rights were finally abolished in 1927. With that the last vestige of rural life left central London.

Whitechapel was also renowned for its Jewish meat market and associated kosher slaughterhouses in the alleyways off the south side of the High Road. Immune from the City's control, the conditions in the mid nineteenth century were appalling. Public health laws closed them down, and the Jews moved out of Whitechapel. Bloom's restaurant is one of the few active reminders of the Hebrew traditions of Whitechapel.

The market tradition also survived. By the 1850s, as cattle-droving dwindled with the arrival of rail transport, the wide unpaved areas in Whitechapel Road, known as the Waste, were being used by street sellers to set up stalls. Whitechapel Waste market has continued to flourish for 130 years. Every day except Sunday about 100 stalls line the wide pavement on the north side. The grand scale of the street, the trees, the market stalls and gabled buildings are its salvation, giving it an almost Parisian feel. On the opposite side is the imposing façade of the London Hospital, built in 1757.

The market sells most things – fruit and veg., clothes, jewellery, rugs and bags and other household items. Henry and Joe Mizler, boxing brothers, have run the fish stall for thirty years, and Ted Willis's flower stall in front of the hospital has a marvellous display. His family business goes back 140 years; his great-grandmother, who smoked a clay pipe and wore lace-up boots, sold flowers from a basket in the City. The market is unusual in that it remains busy until late afternoon, catching workers on their way home.

Mile End Waste is really an extension of Whitechapel, operating on Saturdays only. Many of the traders come from the mid-week lunchtime markets such as Whitecross Street and Leather Lane. The market was established in 1870 when efforts to stamp out sales of clothing failed. Until recently Mile End used to be known for its second-hand furniture, but this has regrettably disappeared. Now it sells mainly cheap pots and pans, china, fabrics and net curtains.

Part of the Waste has been laid out as a garden. Here stand monuments to two great Whitechapel missionaries: William Booth, who founded the Salvation Army in 1865, and Dr Barnardo. Behind the market stalls are the charming Trinity House almshouses built in 1695 on land bequeathed by 'Capt. Hen'y Mudd'! Captain Cook R.N., circumnavigator and explorer, lived opposite at No. 88 Mile End Road.

There is no shortage of drinking holes in Whitechapel and Mile End Roads, which is hardly surprising when there are two breweries, Watney's and Bass Charrington's, in the area. The Blind Beggar next to the Albion brewery is probably the most infamous. It has been tarted up since the Kray brothers murders, but it's still not a place I'd take my grandmother. She might prefer the Whitechapel Art Gallery or the famous old Bell Foundry, neither of which should be missed.

Whitecross Street, EC1

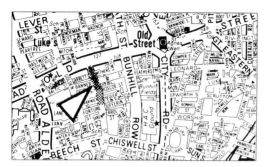

Merchandise: Clothes, food, flowers and novelties.

Opening times: 10.30 a.m. to 2.30 p.m. Monday to Friday.

Location: Whitecross Street from Old Street south to Fortune Street.

Nearest tube: Barbican (Circle, Metropolitan), Old Street (Northern).

Buses: Nos. 5, 55, 243 (Old Street), nos. 4, 279A (Aldersgate Street), nos. 43, 76, 141, 214, 263A, 271 (City Road).

Whitecross Street is one of my favourite markets. Like Leather Lane, Lower Marsh and Strutton Ground it is a lunchtime market, largely serving office workers. Its size is ideal, neither so large that it is a struggle to get through, nor too small to have a good choice. The street itself is narrow, quaint yet unpretentious, and tucked away from the traffic noise of Old Street.

'Whitecruche strete' is mentioned as early as 1226, named after the ancient white stone cross which stood beside 'Eald strete'. Old Street was probably part of the pre-Roman British trackway which skirted the low ground where the Romans built their city. It forded the Thames at Fulham and followed the line of Piccadilly, Theobalds Road, Old Street, Bethnal Green Road, and Roman Road to the old ford crossing of the River Lea.

Whitecross Street led down to the medieval City walls at Cripplegate and was 'replenished with small tenements, cottages and alleys' (Stow). In Elizabethan times it was also famous for Edward Alleyn's Fortune Theatre. Being outside the walls Whitecross Street was a favourite place for travelling pedlars and tinkers, who were not allowed into the City where markets and prices were strictly controlled by the guilds. The promise of bargains lured some folk out to Whitecross Street.

Today the market has more respectability and dignity. The traders are mostly polite and friendly; no one is harangued to buy. Usually there are about 140 stalls selling all manner of useful and everyday things such as towels, electrical goods, shampoo, tinned food, leather bags, tools and magazines. Clothes vary with the season: gloves, hats, mufflers and wellies in winter; shirts, sandals and bikinis in summer. There is a good baker and butcher (Greenwood's) and near by at No. 196 Old Street is Sunwheel, a mecca for wholefood and macrobiotic connoisseurs.

Looking north, the picturesque Victorian shops and houses frame the extraordinary obelisk spire of St Luke's Church, designed by George Dance and still in ruins after the war. The view south is dominated by the towers of the Barbican, four times as high, and the great glass office blocks of the Whitbread redevelopment. Nestling below these are the remnants of the old brewery, which began in 1742. Brewing stopped in 1976. The porter tun room with its 1782 kingpost roof is a magnificent spectacle. The mighty shire dray-horses still clop the streets and pull the Lord Mayor's coach. Whitbread's own all the nearby pubs: the Chiswell Street Vaults are worth seeing but are usually packed; the British Queen and the Two Brewers in Whitecross Street are more basic and serve the locals. The Barbican Arts Centre, with its theatre, concert hall, cinema and art gallery, and the Safeway supermarket at the bottom end of Whitecross Street draw in outsiders, and may gradually bring more evening life, more cafés and wine bars. What one hopes is that the city office blocks are not allowed to destroy this most affable, historic and characterful of market streets.

Part Three

Bayswater Road, W2, and Piccadilly, W1

Merchandise: Paintings, prints, etchings and reproductions.

Opening times: 9.30 a.m. to 4 p.m. Sunday.

Location: South side of Bayswater Road from Albion Gate to Queensway. South side of Piccadilly from Queen's Walk to Hyde Park Corner, and St James's churchyard (Thurs.–Sat.).

Nearest tube: Landcaster Gate (Central), Green Park (Victoria, Piccadilly, Jubilee).

Buses: Nos. 12, 28, 88 (Bayswater Road), nos. 9, 14, 19, 22, 25, 38, 509 (Piccadilly).

This is not one of London's traditional markets and one hopes that the tourists who flock from their Bayswater and Mayfair hotels are not misled into thinking it is. For the tourist it is a poor substitute for Petticoat Lane or Portobello Road. The seemingly endless row of paintings and prints pinned or propped against the park railings is a Parisian idea, copying the stalls on the embankment of the Seine near St Michel. In Paris, although many of the pictures on show are overpriced or mediocre, there is at least a sense of artistic tradition. One can't really say the same about Bayswater or Piccadilly!

Occasionally the eye is caught by a delicate watercolour or a skilful etching, but most of the pictures are crude or uninteresting – hack interpretations of over-exploited London scenes, beefeaters

and horseguards, or vulgar landscapes and portraits of buxom brown-eyed señoritas of the sort Woolworth's sells. There are always hucksters with cheap and nasty souvenirs. People obviously buy them, one supposes to take back to the Texan ranch or Tokyo apartment. The British snap up their equivalent in Benidorm or Amsterdam.

The best thing is the setting, the green backcloth of trees and grass. Green Park is a perfect picture at daffodil time and Kensington Gardens is always a joy, even on a gloomy winter day; nannies pushing prams, little boys flying kites and couples courting. The dip in Bayswater Road is the valley of the River Westbourne, now confined below ground. The bourne rises on the slopes of West Hampstead, where it is called the Kilburn, and flows south marking the boundary between the old manors of Paddington and Notting Hill. The Westbourne feeds the Serpentine which was dammed in 1730 as part of the grandiose landscaping for the grounds of Kensington Palace. Today there are neat dark-green notices on the wall to Kensington Palace: NO PAINTINGS TO BE HUNG ON THESE RAILINGS. I can see why.

Eastwards along Piccadilly on Thursdays to Saturdays the enterprising craft market in the yard of Wren's St James's Church is charming and friendly, with an excellent coffee shop to boot.

Bell Street, NW1

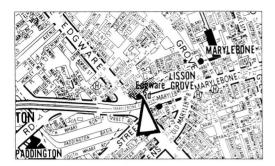

Merchandise: Second-hand books, clothes, furniture and junk.

Opening times: 9 a.m. to 5 p.m. Saturday.

Location: Western end of Bell Street, from Edgware Road to Lisson Street.

Nearest tube: Edgware Road (District, Metropolitan, Bakerloo).

Buses: Nos. 6, 8, 16, 16A, 159, 172.

Bell Street is a charming relic of old working-class Marylebone, a little backwater which progress has passed by. The shabby Saturday market is a part of this character, one of London's genuine second-hand junk markets.

Three hundred years ago Bell Street was a narrow lane crossing Bell Field from Lisson Green to Edgware Road. The field belonged to the Bell Inn which fed off the coaching trade on the main road. Edgware Road, the old A5, was a turnpike road which ran from Tyburn gallows (now Marble Arch) to St Albans and the north-west.

Bell Street today remains quiet while the world thunders along Edgware Road and over the flyover to the Westway. Usually about thirty stalls are sprinkled along the street. No licences are required; anyone can set up and pay on the day. At the Edgware Road end beside the Green Man a flower-seller and greengrocer do a brisk trade. The rest of the market is a strange concoction of tatty third-hand clothes, pre-war radio sets, old mangles, dilapidated armchairs, dusty piles of books and jumble. Browsers shuffle from stall to stall, sifting or gazing and occasionally mumbling a question to the vendor. It is rather like the poor end of Portobello Road or Westmoreland Road, only more sedate. Greer Books at No. 87 Bell Street is delightfully Dickensian, so full of antiquarian books that you can hardly squeeze inside the shop. Further along beyond the market is Bell Street Bikes, one of London's friendlier bicycle shops.

Bell Street gives the appearance of being in decline, but I'm not sure that it has ever been particularly lively or noisy – nor would one want it to be. Edgware Road with its hi-fi and electrical enthusiasts searching for components is busy, modern and neon. Pedestrians scuttle towards Church Street market up the road; few turn to look down Bell Street.

Bermondsey, SE1

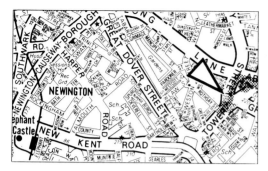

Merchandise: Antiques, furniture, ceramics, silver.

Opening times: 7 a.m. to 5 p.m. (officially, but often starts and finishes earlier) Friday.

Location: Bermondsey Square, Abbey Street, Bermondsey Street and Tower Bridge Road.

Nearest tube: Borough (Northern), Elephant and Castle (Bakerloo).

Buses: Nos. 1, 42, 78, 188.

Bermondsey market, known also as the New Caledonian market, is the main dealers' market for antiques in London and for middlemen from all over southern England. The standard of goods is high and exclusively antique, with none of the modern crafts, clothing or trinket trade which pervades so many of London's markets. Most of the goods are Victorian – furniture, objets d'art and high-class bric-à-brac.

Trading starts very early on a Friday morning, usually by 5 a.m. Furniture is often exchanged by dealers even earlier. Antiques arriving by van from provincial auction rooms may be transferred by torchlight at 3 a.m. to a waiting lorry in Bermondsey Street which will speed to catch the first Channel ferry for quick sale in Italy or Germany. Bermondsey market is big business.

Bermondsey is a dilapidated part of south London. Forty years ago it was an impoverished working-class community between the Surrey docks and central London. That community disappeared as the docks closed. The desolation of Bermondsey is relieved only on a Friday morning, and then it is mainly by foreigners from north of the river.

Bermondsey was a curious choice for relocating the Caledonian market after the war. The Old Caledonian had opened in 1855 on a spacious site, one mile square, at Copenhagen Fields in Islington. Originally it was a cattle market, a replacement for Smithfield, but by 1890 a junk market had become established on Fridays. Islington, as the first stop from London up the Great North Road, has always been a rallying point for pedlars and tinkers, but the market had its heyday in the twenties and thirties. From 1924 the junk market operated on Tuesdays as well as Fridays. There was a toll system for entry – poor traders just paid the entry fee carrying what they could sell, spreading out their wares on the ground. Proper stalls cost more, and the plum pitches were won by runners who sprinted ahead when the gates opened to reserve a prime spot. From here the 'silver kings' operated in style; the

Caledonian market, 1936, painted by Harry Morley (Museum of London)

rest was crammed with hucksters, cheap-jacks and junk men. All around were the driftwood and wreckage of a thousand lives: door knobs, bicycle wheels, broken mirrors and vague pieces of rusty iron, whose mission in life Time had obliterated. Yet in those days more antiques were picked up for a song there than anywhere since. Walter Sickert thought the Caledonian market his idea of heaven. On a good day over 100,000 people flocked to the market. It was a feature of the London calendar and its closure in 1939 was a great loss. Three of the huge corner pubs, the clock tower and the massive wrought-iron railings still survive.

The New Caledonian market at Bermondsey opened in May 1949 on land flattened by bombs. Only a quarter of the houses in Bermondsey Square were left, on the site of the old abbey cloisters. After a slow start Bermondsey has grown to such an extent that there is now a five-year waiting list for one of the 270 stalls. The links with Islington are very dim now; not only does it lack the space of Copenhagen Fields but the character is also different. The Old Caledonian market had a reputation for the easy disposal of stolen goods; Bermondsey is middle class, respectable and commercial. There are fewer cockney voices to be heard now. The 'knockers' and 'totters' who collected door to door have little joy these days. The value of antiques is too well known; Victorian oddments, once the knockers' daily trade, fetch high prices in fashionable shops.

The early start and uninviting location ensure that the market is still mainly for dealers. However, Bermondsey is adjusting more to the general public. Dealers' trading is finished by 9 a.m. and, although some stalls pack up, other traders then take their

Aerial view of the old 'Cally' in full cry, looking south-east. The clock tower is now in the middle of a park (G.L.C.)

place. Bermondsey's reputation for reasonable prices has spread. Increasingly, American tourists who flock to Portobello Road and Camden Passage are hearing of Bermondsey. By ten o'clock tourists and private buyers outnumber the pros, rummaging through the closely packed rows of stalls. Stallholders sit back and deal with the visitors and no longer combine the conflicting demands of selling and searching other stalls for bargains.

For those seeking refreshment Bill's van in the square next to the densest mass of stalls serves an inexhaustible stream of tea, coffee, hot dogs and good humour from dawn to noon. The Market Café in Tower Bridge Road and Rose's Dining Rooms in Bermondsey Street north of Long Lane serve greasy breakfasts, and for those who require sterner stuff, the Hand and Marigold on the corner of Bermondsey Street and Cluny Place is open from 7.30 a.m. on Fridays. South of the Hand and Marigold, beyond Decima Place, is a small and much older general street market selling fruit, veg. and flowers – useful if you are tired of antiques.

Camden Lock, NW1

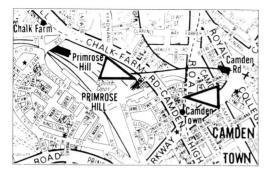

Merchandise: Crafts and cottage industry products.

Opening times: 10 a.m. to 6 p.m. Saturday and Sunday.

Location: Commercial Place on the west side of Chalk Farm Road between the canal and railway viaduct. Overspill on to the corner of Buck Street and Camden High Street.

Nearest tube: Camden Town (Northern).

Buses: Nos. 24, 27, 29, 31, 68, 74, 134, 168, 214, 253.

Camden Lock is a success story of renovation and rejuvenation. Before 1972 it was a disused timber wharf, a ramshackle collection of old warehouses beside the Regent's Canal. The first phase of restoration created a cluster of workshops which were opened in 1973. Among the first tenants were a brave group of five female Hornsey College art students making jewellery. The workshops rapidly became an attractive colony for artists and craftsmen, potters, sculptors, painters, cabinet-makers and leather-workers, attracting colour-supplement publicity. The scheme won a conservation award in 1976.

The crafts market opened in March 1974 on the waste ground immediately next to the road north of the canal bridge. At first on Saturdays, but before long on Sundays too, the market has thrived. The idea of making things and selling them at a market is back in fashion; 'small is beautiful' seems to be here to stay. About 200 stalls pack into the limited space and line Commercial Place alongside the railway viaduct. There are all manner of crafts – candles, silverware, ethnic jewellery, printed scarves, Indian beads, pottery, home-made chocolates and cakes, toys, belts and badges proclaiming 'Gay whales against racism'.

There is the backcloth of Dingwall's Dance Hall and chic restaurants like the Lock Stock and Barrel and Le Routier, and the water where the Fair Lady and the Jenny Wren offer canal cruises. It is all very relaxed and pleasantly informal – cobbles, barges, old brick and timber-clad warehouses and tiled roofs. Not that Camden Lock has survived without a battle; Northside Developments Ltd, who own the land, and the British Waterways Board have repeatedly proposed redevelopment for offices and studios and a smaller formal covered market. Colonel Siefert's plans have been vigorously fought by the Camden Lock Tenants' Association, so far successfully, but it will be a very long war of attrition.

The Lock attracts huge crowds of browsers and many tourists. A hundred yards south of the canal bridge on the other side of the road is Camden Antique Market which, despite its name, is an extension of Camden Lock's crafts market, open at the weekend. North of the railway Chalk Farm Road has been taken over and transformed by the antique trade, selling up-market furniture and objets d'art, no doubt a spin-off from the clientele of the Lock. Most of the shops open on Sundays, including the Chalk Farm Nutrition Centre at No. 40 which offers goats' cheese, 200 kinds of herbs and all the normal health foods and remedies. Opposite the shops another fleamarket has swamped the yard, ramps and insides of the Old Stables, formerly a horse hospital. The Canal market just east of the High Street bridge is yet another overflow for the insatiable Camden Lock boom.

Inverness Street market is near enough to bring you back to earth and the Hawley Arms over the road in Castlehaven Road is rough and ready despite its provincial beers. I still like Marine Ices opposite the Roundhouse for their cheap Italian food and delectable ice cream. It fits the Camden Town style.

Camden Passage, N1

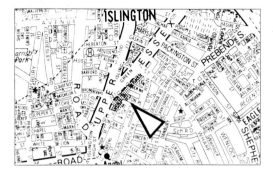

Merchandise: Antiques, objets d'art, jewellery, books.

Opening times: 10 a.m. to 2 p.m. Wednesday. 10 a.m. to 5 p.m. Saturday.

Location: Camden Passage, between Islington Green and Islington High Street, Pierrepont Row and Charlton Place.

Nearest tube: Angel (Northern).

Buses: Nos. 4, 19, 30, 38, 43, 73, 171, 263A, 277, 279 (Upper Street).

Set in an old street of great charm, the Camden Passage antique market is itself not as old as one might think, having been established for only thirty years. With Bermondsey and Portobello it is one of London's most important outdoor antique markets.

Camden Passage is a curious name for Islington, not to be confused with Camden Lock at Camden Town. Once known as Cumberland Row, it was renamed in 1876 after Charles Pratt, the first Earl of Camden, who had owned the land. For centuries people have been coming to Islington for its pleasures or through it on their way north. In the 1920s Camden Passage was known to visitors of Collins' Music Hall in Islington Green. The young Charlie Chaplin used to be taken to see the toy shop at the north end of Camden Passage by Kate Carney who was a regular performer at Collins'. In those days the Passage was like a narrow village street, lined with ordinary local shops and houses.

Through the 1950s the Angel Islington maintained its poor Monopoly-board reputation as a down-at-heel working-class area. Just a few enlightened house buyers were beginning to recognize the incredible potential of Islington's Georgian squares and terraces. Houses which now sell for £300,000 were going for £2,000. In 1958 an antique shop was opened in Camden Passage by Leigh Underhill. The seed was sown: since then Islington has become fashionable and Camden Passage has boomed.

The market was established in 1960 by John Friend who lived in Phelps Cottage. On his initiative the awnings were erected in Pierrepont Row and Charlton Place. The surge of interest in antiques through the sixties and seventies, coupled with Islington's rise in prosperity, ensured the success of the market and changed the old character of the Passage. In the early seventies the Galleries were built out of a disused warehouse at the north end of Camden Passage with a black glass canopy for the open market which fronts Islington Green. It is now called 'the Georgian Village', a somewhat

pretentious name. More recently the old tramshed at the south end of Camden Passage has been cleaned and converted into antique shops, a welcome improvement although again its name, 'The Mall', is unimaginative; why not 'The Tramshed'?

The market has an ordered gentility which is different from most street markets. Jewellery, objets d'art, books, old postcards, and bric-à-brac are carefully laid out on trestle tables beneath the various awnings and arcades. Real bargains are hard to find. The prices tend to match the up-market clientele and tourists who converge here in the summer. As an antique centre the shops are as important as the stalls, specializing in furniture, Art Nouveau and Art Deco, porcelain, clocks, prints, maps and watercolours, silver and Victorian toys. Antique shops have spread up Essex Road and Upper Street replacing many of the traditional local shops. The most recent expansion is another thirty-five stalls on to the Green itself, sheltering under the giant plane trees.

Camden Passage's other claim to fame is its restaurants. Frederick's, Monsieur Frog's, Uppers and Aquilino's are old favourites fitting a range of tastes and purses, sadly outnumbered by new brash pizza parlours. As for pubs, the Camden Head is popular and worth a visit for its genuine Victorian acid-etched glass and mirrors, if not for its beer. For a quality pint a ten-minute walk takes the connoisseur to the Crown in Cloudesley Road, the Empress of Russia in St John Street or the Island Queen in Noel Road.

The conversion of Camden Passage from a dowdy local shopping street to an expensive and fashionable antique centre is virtually complete. The character now is threatened by the slick whims of shopfitters and the ambitions of landowners who want to build extra floors and to cover every untouched corner, like Pierrepont Row. On the other hand the prosperity of the new shops and restaurants is a security against more radical change. The magnificent underground public convenience in Islington High Street where a former attendant kept goldfish in the glass tanks above the marble and brass urinals was shut so that the road could be widened. With huge office blocks rising all round the Angel junction, Camden Passage should count its blessings. The ghost of Charlie Chaplin might not be able to find his toy shop, but at least he might recognize the street.

Chalton Street, NW1

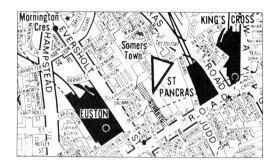

Merchandise: Clothes, fabrics and household goods.

Opening times: Noon to 2.30 p.m. Monday to Friday (but busy only Friday).

Location: Chalton Street, between Euston Road and Phoenix Road.

Nearest tube: Euston (Northern, Victoria), King's Cross (Piccadilly, Metropolitan, Circle).

Buses: Nos. 14, 18, 30, 73, 77A.

Sandwiched between Euston and St Pancras stations, and bounded on the south by Euston Road with its hellish noise of lorries, Chalton Street runs north through that curious area, Somers Town. It is a forgotten quarter, largely ignored by recent redevelopment, with decaying fragments of seedy Regency terraces and quiet shabby streets. Chalton Street is now a backwater, once the heart of a vibrant community: the Brill was one of London's rowdiest Friday and Saturday night markets.

Chalton Street market stutters into life on Friday at lunchtime when perhaps eighty stalls sell clothes, shoes, houseplants, cheap jewellery and electric sockets. There is no attempt to compete with Chapel Market up at Islington for fruit and vegetables. The clientele is largely female office workers from Euston Road.

Apart from Stagnells at No. 28 where cheery dears sell you sticky cakes and pull your leg, few of the shops have much to offer. Some of the side turnings look more tempting, particularly Churchway which leads through to yet quieter back streets. The Somers Town Coffee House has a nice name but little else to recommend it as a pub. The Rising Sun on the corner with Euston Road is rich with mirrors, mahogany and old photographs and has been done up recently by Ind Coope (alias Taylor Walker). It does well at lunchtime.

Immediately east is the Shaw Theatre, and just beyond that the site for the new British Library. With the dozens of glass and concrete blocks lining Euston Road one wonders how long it will be before Chalton Street and Churchway disappear and Somers Town becomes completely forgotten.

Columbia Road, E2

Merchandise: Flowers, pot plants, shrubs, garden accessories.

Opening times: 8 a.m. to 12.30 p.m. Sunday.

Location: Columbia Road east of Ravenscroft Street.

Nearest tube: Old Street (Northern).

Buses: Nos. 6, 35, 55 (Hackney Road).

The Sunday morning flower and plant market in Columbia Road is a delightful place. This quaint street with its little two-storey terraces and lovely wooden shopfronts is a gem. Not many people know the market; it is tucked away protected from casual trade by backstreets, remote from the tumult and loafing hordes of Brick Lane or Petticoat Lane.

Usually there are about twenty stalls selling all manner of cut flowers, garden shrubs, spring bulbs, houseplants, nursery trees, herbs and seeds. Several barrows specialize in fertilizers and compost or, like Bill and Ben, sell terracotta flower pots and ornate chimney pots to decorate the patio. At Christmas time there are laurel wreaths and rows of Christmas trees of all sizes, miniature for the front parlour window and tall for the office foyer. A vivid display of artificial and dried flowers decks one stall, brightly painted teasels and pampas like ostrich feathers. It is a colourful scene; everyone is friendly and good-natured.

There is a collection of original Victorian shop-fronts on the south-east side of the street which is remarkable. Presumably there has not been the cheap money or rapidly gained affluence which might have ripped out the old slatted shutters and timber stallrisers, and installed aluminium, glass and garish tiles instead. Nor should this ever be allowed to happen.

The flower market has been here for about sixty years. Until 1960 it lay in the shadow of one of the great philanthropic white elephants of the

By the First World War the Columbia market was derelict and disintegrating, a playground for local children (G.L.C.)

Victorian era, the Columbia market. Baroness Burdett-Coutts, a lady of means and conscience, provided £200,000 for the two-acre site, formerly slums, and for construction. The design by H. A. Darbyshire was as ornate as the Natural History Museum, a magnificent Gothic monument, with pinnacles and spires, stone-vaulted roof, traceried windows and stained glass worthy of a cathedral. The opening on 28 April 1869 was a pompous affair, complete with the Archbishop of Canterbury and the Duke of Wellington.

The intention was laudable: to provide the impoverished East End costermongers with a con-venient sheltered market with stables, storage and uplifting surroundings. It was a flop from the first day. Wholesalers were reluctant to direct supplies from existing markets and the street traders were loath to leave their barrows in the gutter. Futile attempts were made to convert the deserted build-ing into a fish and meat market, and later into workshops. In 1960 this desolate relic of a Victorian ideal was demolished, leaving only the cast-iron railings beside Baroness Road. These too have gone now and the site is covered with municipal flats. It is a stern example to those who wish to impose their dreams on society.

Exmouth Market, EC1

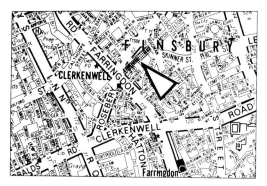

Merchandise: Second-hand books, bric-à-brac, clothes.

Opening times: 9.30 a.m. to 4.00 p.m. Tuesday and Friday (some stalls other days also).

Location: Exmouth Market, between Farringdon Road and Rosoman Street.

Nearest tube: Farringdon (Circle, Metropolitan).

Buses: Nos. 19, 38, 63, 171, 196, 221, 259.

Exmouth Market, like the rest of Clerkenwell, is enjoying something of a renaissance. Between 1945 and 1980 the accumulation of slum clearance, war damage, closure of factories and the lure of the suburbs had reduced the local population to a tiny fraction of what it was sixty years ago; Exmouth Market had become a ghostly and shabby backwater.

With the efforts of a few enthusiastic Council officials and the Angel Improvement Trust the market was relaunched in 1986. Today, with the whole street attractively paved, many of the buildings cleaned and most of the empty shops reoccupied, it has an altogether more promising future, with fifty stalls specializing in second-hand books, odds and ends and clothes. Only the shellfish stall and fruit barrow survive from the old days. Chapel Market and Leather Lane are close enough to capture most of the custom for daily nutritional and household requirements. Now people go to Exmouth Market to browse and amble.

The market attracts lunchtime workers from the new zappy businesses which colonize Clerkenwell and sorters from Mount Pleasant across the road.

A wide range of restaurants and cafés have sprung up in the street, recalling the time 200 years ago when Clerkenwell was famous for its spas like Sadler's Wells and Merlin's Cave. Exmouth Street, formerly known as Baynes Row, was then a track across the fields leading to the London Spa Tavern where 'Spaw Ale' and roast pork topped the menu.

The market existed by 1850. By then the spas had disappeared, the wild flowers and fresh air replaced by sweatshops and workhouses making artificial flowers and clothing, alongside the metal-platers, watchmakers and distillers. Clerkenwell's teeming population was crammed into tight terraces and tenements. Rosebery Avenue was built in 1891, removing through traffic from Exmouth Street. The market attracted hordes of street sellers and small shops. Lumley's the pastry cooks sold penny meat pies, and Mehew's made boiled suet and currant pudding. Husband and wife often quarrelled and threw slabs of pudding at each other! Travelling players and Punch and Judy shows entertained crowds of wide-eyed children. An old soldier from the Zulu war told them tales of his battles, conjured potatoes and live rabbits from his empty hat and finally, with a long razor-sharp sword, sliced the potato in half on the open palm of his blind-folded wife.

The soldier and most of the old shops have long gone, but there are still reminders that Clerkenwell used to be London's 'Little Italy', once a ghetto for Italian immigrants. In the last century Joe Grimaldi, the legendary but tragic clown, lived in Exmouth Street. Still today the lofty Italian campanile of the Church of the Holy Redeemer dominates the street, the interior as 'high' as the Church of England will allow. After the war many Italian ex-prisoners stayed on and converged on Clerkenwell, their traditional home, where they still run the cafés, like Brivati's and Boggi's. At No. 167 Farringdon Road Gazzano's have sold parmesan, prosciutto, pasta and chianti for four generations. The annual Italian procession from the Italian St Peter's church in Clerkenwell Road every July is not to be missed, ending in a carnival on Clerkenwell Green.

Farringdon Road, EC1

Merchandise: Second-hand books and manuscripts.

Opening times: 6 a.m. to 2 p.m. Monday to Friday, weather permitting.

Location: Farringdon Road, between Clerkenwell Road and Cowcross Street.

Nearest tube: Farringdon (Circle, Metropolitan).

Buses: Nos. 5, 55, 243 (Clerkenwell Road), nos. 63, 221, 259 (Farringdon Road).

This is one of London's smallest and most specialized markets, and has a curious history, being close to the great Smithfield meat market and the old Fleet and Farringdon markets. Until the mid nineteenth century this area was one of London's most notorious slums or 'rookeries', a maze of courts and alleys beside the Fleet River which flowed south to meet the Thames at Blackfriars. In 1856 Farringdon Street and Farringdon Road swept away the slums and the old Fleet market which had sold fruit, vegetables and fish. The Farringdon Street market replaced it but despite being the pitch of Mayhew's celebrated watercress-sellers it soon became a poor affair, 'a melancholy intermingling of closed shops and stalls', and closed by 1880.

However, soon after the opening of the Holborn Viaduct in 1869 a new street market was started in Farringdon Road, by a Mr James Dabbs. It rapidly became a mecca for dealers in second-hand books. Perhaps Dabbs was attracted by the numerous literary associations near by: Christ's Hospital where Coleridge and Charles Lamb were at school, the residences of Dr Johnson and Goldsmith,

Richard Savage's birthplace, and the Charterhouse where Thackeray had been a schoolboy.

Until twenty years ago the daily market dealt not only in books, maps and prints but also nails, brushes, tools and hardware odds and ends. Since then it has declined. The setting has been ruined by traffic, the incessant rumble of huge lorries, the sickly smell of diesel fumes. The street is grey and dismal, with the long grimy brick wall hiding the Metropolitan line (the world's first underground railway) in its cutting, the now demolished goods depot which was once its terminus, and forbidding commercial buildings which line the other side of Farringdon Road, the tail end of Fleet Street, home of the *Daily Worker* and *Morning Star*.

Graham Greene sums up the market:

> There is something Victorian about the whole place – an air of ugly commercial endeavour mixed with old idealism and philanthropies. It isn't only the jumble of unattractive titles on the dusty spines, the huge weight of morality at sixpence a time, even the setting has an earnestness . . . The public houses are like a lesson in temperance. ('George Moore and Others' from *Collected Essays*.)

Today there are rarely more than half a dozen stalls, with keen browsers thumbing through rows of faded titles, craning their necks in a sideways tilt, a tatterdemalion market of the unwanted. Its survival would please Mr Dabbs, and is due to Mr Jeffery who runs all the stalls. It is worth a visit if you like old books, and for valuable chance bargains. If the traffic depresses you too much then you are just a short walk from Leather Lane.

Gabriel's Wharf and Riverside Walk, SE1

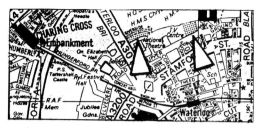

Merchandise: Crafts, jewellery, second-hand books.

Opening times: Gabriel's Wharf – 9.30 a.m. to 6 p.m. Friday, Saturday and Sunday. Riverside book market – 12 to 7 p.m. Saturday and Sunday.

Location: Gabriel's Wharf, north side of Upper Ground east of LWT Building; Riverside Walk, in front of NFT.

Nearest tube: Waterloo (Northern, Bakerloo).

Buses: Nos. 1, 4, 5, 68, 70, 76, 149, 168, 171, 176, 177, 188.

The birth of the South Bank has been long and painful, dating back to the post-war Festival of Britain. It has taken years for the uncompromising concrete buildings, ramps and stairways to become accepted as 'user-friendly' and for all the jigsaw pieces to be slotted together; it has taken time for the spindly trees to grow and for the urban landscape to mature. The establishment of two new markets on the South Bank is an encouraging sign of diversity and small-scale innovation.

Gabriel's Wharf, between the LWT and Oxo towers, was opened in March 1988, very much in the Camden Lock mould. The cleverly painted mural on the factory wall provides an effective if twee backdrop for the craft bazaar focused around the band-stand, where hired groups play jazz and gentle rock. The traders sell ethnic jewellery, Turkish khilims and rugs, pottery, basketwork and health foods, and the Studio 6 café is friendly and comfortable. Like all new ventures it will gradually get known. Who would have imagined the crowds of Camden Lock back in 1974?

The riverside setting has everything in its favour – the ebb and flow of the tide, the fabulous views across the water to the Temple, the Savoy and the City, and the increasing attractiveness of the Riverside Walk itself. The new Coin Street housing, the refurbishment of the Oxo Building and the Museum of the Moving Image will all help. Jubilee Gardens and the new open space next to Gabriel's Wharf are well used.

In front of the National Film Theatre cafeteria, cunningly sheltering from the elements under Waterloo Bridge, the book market on Riverside Walk has quite a Parisian flavour – sagging trestle tables groaning under the weight of books and flap-down lockable stores. The books displayed are well above jumble-sale prices, not give-aways, but it has become a venue for browsers, buskers and imbibers every weekend. Film, concert, theatre and exhibition buffs now have more reason to loiter on the South Bank, and to realize the distant dream of 1951.

GABRIEL'S
WHARF
MARKET
▶▶▶▶

Greenwich, SE10

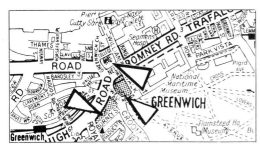

Merchandise: Crafts, antiques, second-hand books, wholesale vegetables.

Opening times: 9 a.m. to 6 p.m. Saturday and Sunday; wholesale market 6 a.m. to noon Monday to Friday.

Location: Entrance on south side of College Approach; also north side of Stockwell Street and corner of High Road and Royal Hill.

Nearest railway station: Greenwich (London Bridge).

Buses: Nos. 1, 77, 180, 188, 286.

The first edition of this book featured Greenwich market under the wholesale section, with a subsidiary mention of a new antique market. Now the roles are reversed, such is the speed of change: the wholesale vegetable market has shrivelled and the craft and antique trade has flourished to take its place and more besides.

The 1981 report by the Ministry of Agriculture, Fisheries and Food urged that by 1991 London would need only three wholesale fruit and vegetable markets. Greenwich would be one of those to go. Even the L.C.C. report in 1896 suggested that business was diminishing except during a strawberry glut; Kent farmers received better prices at Borough. So it has proved: only a few salesmen remain in a corner of the old market. Rowe, Manchett and Till survive, but also operate at Borough Market. The rustic charm of straw on cobbles, the earthy smell of fresh vegetables, and the granite setts stained with the juice of squashed tomatoes and oranges have all gone. Now a different trade

keeps the Greenwich market story alive.

A charter was first granted in 1700 to the Earl of Romney, who then vested it in the Commissioners of Greenwich Hospital. The market was held where the Dreadnought Seamen's Hospital stands now. In the 1820s the medieval core of Greenwich Village vanished completely, and the Greenwich Hospital Improvement Act enabled its surveyor, Joseph Kay, to lay out Nelson Road, College Approach and King William Walk with handsome Regency terraces, including a new site for Greenwich market, complete with stables and warehouses. The 1849 By-laws limited produce to vegetables, fruits, roots, seeds, plants and earthenware. The market was crowded with horses, farmers' wagons and Greenwich fishermen selling oysters and whitebait; tinkers and pedlars infested the alleys. Penalties were imposed on all other stalls within Greenwich parish. Even street hawkers had to pay market tolls, until the Hospital intervened in 1880 and repealed this ludicrous clause. No sizeable street market ever took root in Greenwich. The half-dozen surviving fruit

and vegetable stalls in Earlswood, Tyler and Columb Streets off Trafalgar Road were the nearest thing.

The Hospital still owns the site, now taking rent rather than tolls and stallage. Even under the modern functional canopy the character is delightful. The Grecian-colonnaded entrance from College Approach dates from 1831, with its quaintly moralistic inscription for those departing: A FALSE BALANCE IS ABOMINATION TO THE THE LORD, BUT A JUST WEIGHT IS HIS DELIGHT. From 1845 the large room over the archway was a music hall attached to the Admiral Hardy Tavern next door. Now on Saturdays and Sundays the cobbles are covered with craft stalls, selling papier-mâché jewellery boxes, pot-pourri, framed prints, boaters and fedoras, chocolates, dried flowers, polished stones and fossils, all very middle class and respectable. Perhaps it's rather like a National Trust shop, but then, this is Greenwich, honey-pot for tourists and trippers, home of the *Cutty Sark* and the National Maritime Museum. Speciality shops have replaced the vegetable warehouses; boutiques, souvenirs and posh wine bars have usurped the local greengrocers who once bought off the market. Behind the market the cobbles and gutters merge with the alleyways and gift shops of Turnpin Lane and Durnford Passage.

The weekend antique market is on two sites, separated by the new Hotel Ibis on the corner of Greenwich High Road and Stockwell Street. West of the hotel, fifty trestle tables fill the paved area selling coins, medals, china, postage stamps and Dinky toys. Beside the railway cutting in Stockwell Street the range is different – a second-hand record stall blaring Bob Dylan classics, cracked crockery, dusty candlesticks and Victoriana, and furniture at the back. The indoor book market is excellent cover against the rain, and a good place to thumb through the spines of a thousand old tomes. Prices in Greenwich are no longer cheap; enthusiastic amateurs are now outnumbered by shrewd dealers. For refreshment try the Mitre next to St Alphege's church or the Admiral Hardy, which retains its back door into the covered market.

Hackney Stadium, E15

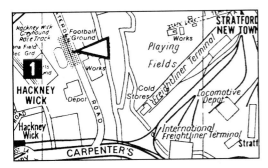

Merchandise: Clothes, household goods, plants, electrical appliances, junk.

Opening times: 6 a.m. to noon Sunday.

Location: Waterden Road in Stadium car-park.

Nearest tube and station: Leyton (Central), Hackney Wick (B.R.).

Buses: Nos. 6, 30, 236, 276, 299.

If you are a speedway or greyhound fan you will know Hackney Stadium. If not then you are unlikely to be familiar with this weird corner of east London, down beside the marshes and Lea navigation at Hackney Wick. Unless, that is, you frequent the Sunday morning market in front of the Stadium in Waterden Road. In keeping with the craze for car-boot sales which have sprung up on privately owned land, Hackney Stadium market attracts shady dealers and rum customers. Nobody here is licensed; you buy at your own risk, the police stay well away. Fly pitchers and hawkers sell different stuff each week. If you know what you are about there are terrific bargains to be had. No doubt a lot of the goods are seconds or off the backs of lorries. Don't ask too many questions.

Hackney Wick is not well served by public transport. Go by car if you can; parking is no problem. Whatever the drawbacks of its location the market certainly attracts the crowds, people from all over London sniffing a cheap snip. The high, shabby grandstands of the Stadium lend an odd and unfriendly background. Nobody hangs around after the market has closed. The pavements soon revert to being bleak and windswept, the rusting chain-link fencing clogged with ancient rotting litter, the verges dirty and dusty. Apart from the hot-dog and tea stand in the market there is nothing much for refreshment locally. Aim for the Falcon and Firkin in Victoria Park Road, or walk up the Lea towpath to the Prince of Wales on Lea Bridge Road.

Kilburn Square, NW6

Merchandise: Mainly clothes, fashion wear, jeans, materials.

Opening times: 9 a.m. to 5 p.m. Friday and Saturday.

Location: West side of Kilburn High Road, opposite Quex Road.

Nearest tube: Kilburn Park (Bakerloo).

Buses: Nos. 8, 16, 28, 31, 32, 172.

This is not a market to travel a long way for, but it relieves the monotony of the run-of-the-mill shops in Kilburn High Road. Slightly set back from the road, forty stalls cluster in the middle of a paved square surrounded by a rather drab 1970s housing development clad in white tiles with ground-floor shops. The wide expanse of pavement affords some respite from the grinding traffic.

Nearly all the stalls sell clothes or materials, including cut-price jeans, fashion blouses and skirts, T-shirts, net curtains and gaudy dress fabrics. The majority of traders are Asians and most of the punters Irish or West Indians. On the litter-ridden pavements Militant Tendency supporters flog their newspapers outside the Irish banks, while drunks totter to or from Biddy Mulligan's. The estate agents like to call this area West Hampstead or Brondesbury, but Kilburn remains determinedly Kilburn, the eastern fringe of Brent. It's a quarter-mile hike south along the High Road to find a decent pint of Young's at the Queen's Arms, passing on the way the solitary fruit and veg. stalls on the corners of Birchington Road, Brondesbury Road, Brondesbury Villas and West End Lane. They provide some colour and banter, and some good bargains.

Kingsland Waste, E8

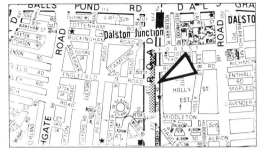

Merchandise: Tools, do-it-yourself materials, timber, electrical spares, hardware, some clothes and food.

Opening times: 9 a.m. to 5 p.m. Saturdays only.

Location: East side of Kingsland Road from Middleton Road to Forest Road.

Nearest railway station: Dalston Junction (Broad Street).

Buses: Nos. 22, 48, 67, 149, 243.

Kingsland Waste market, held only on Saturdays, is a curious affair. It is primarily a non-food market and many of the hundred or so stalls specialize in do-it-yourself hardware. It was the same fifty years ago when the Waste was a good place to pick up spare parts for wirelesses, lawnmowers and bicycles.

There are a dozen stalls selling tools, often at very competitive prices. If you know what you are looking for there is good quality to be found, as well as cheap new Taiwan or Pakistan spanner sets. Other stalls specialize in paint, nuts and bolts, door locks, electrical wire, bicycle wheels, picture frames and watch straps. One stall deals in cameras; a few

enthusiasts gaze at the rather lonely objects, fiddling with shutter mechanisms or peering through lenses and viewfinders. Most of the remaining stalls sell clothes – the ubiquitous range of imported shirts, dresses and coats.

The market occupies the wide pavement and service road with three parallel lines of stalls. Kingsland Road is a very old thoroughfare, originally the Roman road north from Bishopsgate and later a cattle drovers' road and a turnpike. As at Whitechapel the taverns and early nineteenth-century houses were set well back from the muddy highway. The waste land was owned by the Rector of Dalston as part of his glebe and the manorial rights prevented the encroachment of any buildings. It was an obvious place for a market; by the 1880s there were reports of the new market being 'a great obstructive to the hasty pedestrian'. The open ground was also a regular site for political meetings; during the General Strike, when the Labour movement was strong in Hackney, there were huge assemblies and demonstrations.

The market's specialization in non-food goods probably evolved owing to competition from the nearby Ridley Road market, which expanded in the 1920s. With its great range of fruit and veg. Ridley Road remains an ideal complement to the Waste for the Saturday shopper. The public houses at the north and south end of the market, the Lamb and the Fox, are rather dreary places. The Railway Tavern (Shepherd Neame) in St Jude Street, off Kingsland High Street opposite Ridley Road, repays the brisk walk.

London Silver Vaults, WC2

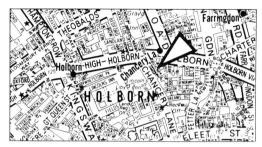

Merchandise: Antique and modern silver, cutlery, plate, coins, jewellery and objets d'art.

Opening times: 9.30 a.m. to 5.30 p.m. Monday to Friday; 9.30 a.m. to 12.30 p.m. Saturday.

Location: Basement of Nos. 53–64 Chancery Lane, entrance in Southampton Buildings.

Nearest tube: Chancery Lane (Central).

Buses: Nos. 8, 17, 18, 22, 25, 45, 46, 171A, 243, 259, 501 (High Holborn).

All that glitters is not gold, as you will discover if you visit the London Silver Vaults. Here is a treasure house as impressive as the crown jewels, an Aladdin's cave of riches and, what is more, open to the public for buying and selling. Just off Chancery Lane in Southampton Buildings you enter an impregnable fortress. Past the security men, the stairwell down to the vaults is caged in thick bars, with portcullises poised to slam shut at a second's warning. No thief could escape. At the bottom the corridor to the vaults twists and turns, with surveillance cameras at every bend.

The London Silver Vaults evolved from the Chancery Lane Safe Deposit Company which began in 1885. Dealers who kept their silver in the strongrooms took clients to the vaults to do business. Here there was peace, quiet and great security. Wartime bombing reinforced this practice and, following the move to the present building in 1953, the Silver Vaults were established as the main silver market in London.

Thirty-three main dealers rent the 150 units of which fifty are shops open for trade, the rest being tiny workrooms and stores, some no bigger than a walk-in cupboard. Each unit is fortified by huge strongroom doors, several feet thick. The cream paint brightens the place but does not hide the hefty defences. Every shop is a marvel of gleaming and shining objects, antique silverware, cutlery, Sheffield plate, Victorian decanters, jewellery, eighteenth-century candlesticks, and silver goblets. The selection is unrivalled throughout the world; the professional knowledge unchallenged.

In the corridor informative plaques tell the

tourist about silver marks such as the Leopard's Head and the Britannia Standard. The Leopard's Head was the first hallmark. Decreed by Edward I in 1300 as the 'King's Mark' it became crowned in 1478 until 1827, since when the uncrowned Leopard's Head has been the distinguishing mark of London silver. Birmingham's Anchor and Sheffield's Crown were wagered for in the Crown and Anchor Tavern in London.

The names of the present-day dealers betray an expected foreign influence – Weiss, Koopman, Gieldman, Urbach, Franks, Stodel and Dubiner – shades of the gnomes of Zurich. The London Silver Vaults are a major market for foreign buyers. The recent renovation enables visitors to browse in congenial surroundings, and the multi-lingual signs make sure nobody can get lost.

It is a strange subterranean world, this rich man's version of Goulston Street. Outside is the changing world of day and night, summer and winter. Near by are the Patent Office, Staple Inn with its higgledy-piggledy Tudor buildings facing Holborn, and the lawyers of Gray's and Lincoln's Inns. Everybody is going about their business; few would suspect the treasure trove in the fairy grotto below.

Nags Head, N7

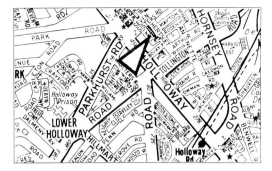

Merchandise: Clothes, new and second-hand, bric-à-brac.

Opening times: 9 a.m. to 5 p.m. Wednesday to Saturday.

Location: South side of Seven Sisters Road, next to Enkel Street.

Nearest tube: Holloway Road (Piccadilly).

Buses: Nos. 4, 14, 17, 19, 29, 43, 45, 153, 221, 253, 259, 263, 271, 279.

Named after the pub on the corner of Holloway Road and Seven Sisters Road, the Nags Head market has existed for about twelve years. Held on empty ground next to Trueform, it sells mainly clothing – denims, blouses, synthetic fur coats, leather jackets, polyester shirts and woollens – an offshoot of the local Cypriot rag trade. The site will eventually be developed for new shops and car parks, perhaps including a permanent market. In the meantime the sixty stalls drop anchor every Wednesday to Saturday behind the daily fruit and veg. stall on Seven Sisters Road.

The market is a small component in this extensive shopping centre: Safeways, Sainsbury's, M. & S. and John Lewis (Jones Bros.) all have large stores. Corrigans at No. 498 Holloway Road and No. 100 Seven Sisters Road are excellent butchers who live up to their reputation. Gibbers at No. 118 Seven Sisters Road are the cheapest greengrocers I know, but beware the marathon queues. The nicest shop is Gerra and Sons at No. 85 Parkhurst Road for everything Italian – cheese, salami, olives, home-made pasta, and always a friendly 'Hello, meesta'.

The worst thing is the traffic. Holloway Road has always been busier than the people who happen to live near by would like. As the way across the hollows between Highgate and Islington it endured huge cattle herds on the hoof to Smithfield and now it bears giant juggernauts seeking the softest route through London. The Victorian street market further down Holloway Road beyond the railway bridge has virtually disappeared; only one or two of the thirty pitches are now occupied regularly.

Bowman Mews opposite the Nags Head market used to lead to Bowman House where Edward Lear the humorist was born in 1812, when the fields were still used for archery. In the mid nineteenth century thousands of terraced houses were built for City clerks, respectable, unpretentious; it was four miles by tram to the Bank of England. Today the Irish dominate the pubs, the Cypriots run the chip shops and the back street car-repair yards, and McDonald's provides the raw material for most of the litter.

A travelling butcher at Holloway

Petticoat Lane, E1

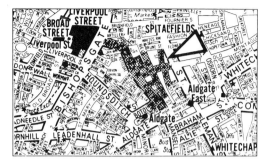

Nearest tube: Aldgate (Metropolitan, Circle), Aldgate East (Metropolitan, District).
Buses: Nos. 5, 10, 15, 22, 25, 40, 42, 44, 67, 78, 225, 253.

Merchandise: Predominantly clothes, but some of most other things. Gold and silver in Goulston Street.

Opening times: Middlesex Street – Sunday morning only. Wentworth Street – 10.30 a.m. to 2.30 p.m. Monday to Friday.

Location: Middlesex Street from Aldgate to Bishopsgate, Goulston Street, Bell Lane, Cobb Street, Leyden Street, Wentworth Street, Toynbee Street and Old Castle Street.

Petticoat Lane is probably London's most famous street market. On a Sunday morning it is London's busiest street, when over a thousand stalls line Middlesex Street and its side turnings and tens of thousands of people push their way through the congested streets, experiencing the atmosphere and hubbub of 'the Lane'.

There has been a market here for over two hundred years. Middlesex Street was once a footpath (known then as Hog Lane) wandering across fields outside the old City walls. In Tudor times fashionable houses were erected, as recounted by Stow: 'In ancient times on both sides of Hog Lane were hedgerows and elm trees, with pleasant fields

Sunday morning in Wentworth Street, 1895, at that time the centre of London's Jewish community (Tower Hamlets Library)

to walk in, insomuch that some gentlemen of the Court and City built their houses here for the air.'

In the seventeenth century the genteel character changed rapidly, being first inundated by refugees after the Great Fire and then saturated with foreign immigrants, particularly French Huguenots and Calvinists in the 1680s. The Huguenot silkweavers and their special skill in making ladies' petticoats gave Petticoat Lane its name.

The market began in the eighteenth century when the French Protestants were pushed north and east towards Bethnal Green and the shops and houses of Petticoat Lane were taken over by Jews. Petticoat Lane is and always has been a market primarily for clothes, with the Jews dealing traditionally in second-hand garments. Petticoat Lane took over from the notorious medieval second-hand clothes market at Rosemary Lane known as Rag Fair. This was where Royal Mint Street is now, close to the Tower of London. It was a dirty and loathsome place where ragged Jews sold rags to penniless poets and parsons. 'By no means belie the name Rag Fair; there is no expressing the poverty of their goods, nor yet their cheapness.' (Cunningham's *Handbook of London*.) Rag Fair had died out by Victorian times, and the last ancient houses were swept away in the 1900s.

Petticoat Lane went from strength to strength, dominated by Jews. In 1851 Mayhew described it as 'two or three miles of old clothes ... a vista of multi-coloured dinginess'. Huge clothes auctions were held in Goulston and Wentworth Streets. The babble of bartering was a mixture of German, Polish, Russian, Hebrew and French, all with Yiddish compounds. Nevertheless the Lane also attracted more visitors from the middle classes than any other market of its day. William Booth disapproved of Petticoat Lane for its trash, cheap garments and ethnic segregation. 'The Jew is the seller and the Gentile the buyer; Petticoat Lane is

the exchange of the Jew but the lounge for the Christian.' The prudish Victorians renamed Petticoat Lane Middlesex Street, being the boundary between the city and Middlesex, very respectable and forgettable.

The Jewish tradition is still surprisingly strong, not just for the Sunday trading and Saturday sabbath. Jews still run much of London's garment trade and 90 per cent of the market stalls still sell clothes. Today nearly all the clothes are new – jeans, leather jackets, fur coats, denim jump-suits, négligées and blouses. Petticoat Lane has been influenced by Carnaby Street and the new boutiques, and now parades the latest fashions and trendy gear. Prices are not necessarily any cheaper than Oxford Street. The huge numbers of visitors, especially tourists in summer, make Petticoat Lane big business. The parking lot off Middlesex Street known as the 'garage' becomes a vast bazaar on Sundays, mainly run by West End dealers. Stallholders are successful and affluent; there is no place here for the dishevelled tramps of Cheshire Street.

The solitary seller is rare in Petticoat Lane. Most stalls have one man or woman shouting out the wares, another serving customers, another handling the money, another organizing stock and maybe another watching for thieves. The Lane has always been known for its pickpockets; if you lose your watch at one end of Petticoat Lane you'll find it on sale when you reach the other. A lot of items fall off the backs of lorries: 'These goods ain't stolen, they just ain't been paid for.'

Besides clothes there are handbags, pots and pans, sham jewellery, novelty toys, roast chestnuts in winter, and a few weekday lunchtime fruit stalls in Wentworth Street. Some of the old Cutler Street gold and coin dealers now congregate on the patch of land at the southern end of Goulston Street.

For refreshment Tubby Isaacs' stall at the south end of the market by Aldgate is famous for its whelks and jellied eels. Bloom's Restaurant at No. 90 Whitechapel High Street serves superb Jewish food, though you need to book for Sundays. If you go north of the market to Artillery Lane, look out for the lovely old shopfront, built in 1756. Bishopsgate is full of pubs of which Dirty Dick's is the most famous but not always the best for beer.

Portobello Road, W10 and W11

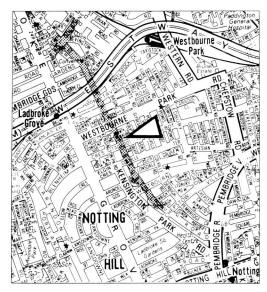

Merchandise: Antiques, bric-à-brac, junk. Also fresh food and clothes.

Opening times: Antiques – 7.00 a.m. to 5.30 p.m. Saturday. Small general market – 9 a.m. to 5 p.m. Monday to Saturday.

Location: Antiques from Chepstow Villas. General market between Lonsdale Road and Tavistock Road. Rags and junk up to Golborne Road. New Portabella Dock, Ladbroke Grove, Sunday.

Nearest tube: Notting Hill Gate (Central, District, Circle), Ladbroke Grove (Metropolitan).

Buses: Nos. 7, 15, 27, 28, 31, 52 (Westbourne Grove), nos. 12, 88 (Notting Hill Gate).

'The world's best-known antique market' and 'London's liveliest street on a Saturday' are fair descriptions of Portobello Road. During the week it is a quiet street, with its crooked terrace houses receding down the hill, shops half open, half closed, and a small sleepy fruit and veg. market north of Lonsdale Road. On Saturday the whole place from Chepstow Villas right up to Golborne Road a mile north is transformed into a seething mass of people and stalls.

Portobello Road has a chequered history. The first house in the street was built in 1850 and called the folly because it stood alone for some years. Before then it had been a country lane leading to Portobello Farm, named by a patriotic farmer after the capture of Porto Bello in the Gulf of Mexico from the Spanish by Admiral Vernon in 1739. By the early 1800s the area had become known as the 'Piggeries' and 'Potteries', occupied by an isolated colony of pig-breeders who lived among their sties. Some reputedly slept with their pigs! Dickens described it as 'a plague spot scarcely equalled in insalubrity by any other part of London'. The smallpox death rate was alarming.

In 1837 the Hippodrome racecourse was laid out west of Portobello Road. Intended as a rival to Ascot and Epsom it was abandoned in 1841. The fields of Portobello Farm were eventually covered in bricks and mortar in 1860. By then house-building for the rich middle classes had outrun demand and this, coupled with the distance from fashionable Bayswater, meant that the houses were either of poor quality or soon divided into lodgings.

The market in Portobello Road grew up in the 1880s in the poorest part of North Kensington. In the 1930s the market was confined to the north end of the road and sold only fruit and vegetables. Antiques had not been heard of in Portobello Road, and until 1939 they were to be found only at the great Caledonian market in Islington.

The antique trade arrived in the late fifties and boomed in the sixties at the same time as Camden Passage got under way. Today, including the covered arcades, over 2,000 antique stallholders operate in Portobello. Although its lively character contributes to the North Kensington community it has outgrown its local function; people come from all over London and beyond.

Chepstow Villas to Lonsdale Road is the smart end, dealing exclusively in antiques. In summer the market creeps into life at dawn. While cars and vans are unloaded and stalls set up, rival experts and West End dealers are already sifting and searching for the unexpected. The dealers know each other's movements, habits and penchants – many will have seen each other the previous morning at Bermondsey. Collector's Corner, one of the oldest

covered arcades on Portobello, opens at 8.30 and rapidly becomes a scrum of bargain hunters.

Back in the fifties collecting antiques was the private hobby of a few eccentrics, not the popular fashion of today. Now it is big business. Many dealers specialize, selling only Edwardian glassware or Persian carpets, late Victorian English porcelain or old lace shawls. One or two characters carry on unchanged: Gypsy Dan, arms tattooed to the elbow, commands a position near Westbourne Park Road, his oddments in deliberate disarray to encourage people to rummage. Meanwhile he props his vast frame on a creaking stool and watches.

The middle section up as far as the Westway flyover is a mixture of bric-à-brac and the weekday food market. On Saturday the fruit stalls expand to take advantage of the huge crowds, some specializing in Caribbean produce. There are good egg, meat and fish stalls, and some excellent shops. Ceres at No. 269 was Britain's prototype wholefood grain shop, and remains terrific value for rice, pulses and grains. Mr Christian's delicatessen in Elgin Crescent caters superbly for the richer palate.

North of Tavistock Road the market is non-food and becomes progressively tattier, degenerating into rag and bones. Bicycle auctions are held under the flyover, viewing at noon, selling at 2 p.m. Countless stalls sell cheap clothes, fake jewellery and quasi-ethnic knick-knacks. A stooping Jewish tailor renovates dinner jackets and tails. The market stutters on up to and into Golborne Road, a shambles of so much junk – all kinds of unwanted domestic scrap which somebody might find useful.

Portobello Road attracts a wide miscellany of people – fading hippies, film stars, punks, old dears in curlers with bags on wheels, Rastafarians and American tourists – all seeking their particular El Dorado. Buskers try their luck, uncoordinated one-man bands, tiresome folkies with droning vocals and strumming guitars, shaven-headed sitar-players and old regulars like Wally, complete with polyphon and parrot. Charles Ives would have loved it. The oldest entertainer in Portobello is the Electric Cinema, one of the first pre-talkies. Portobello Road is an experience, even if you don't set out to buy anything; but like as not you will.

Roman Road, E3

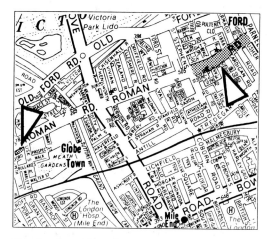

Merchandise: Excellent for clothes and fabrics, particularly discontinued lines and end cuts. Also fresh food and household goods.

Opening times: 8.30 a.m. to 5.30 p.m. Tuesday, Thursday and Saturday.

Location: Eastern end of Roman Road from St Stephen's Road to Parnell Road.

Nearest tube: Mile End (Central, Metropolitan, District).

Buses: Nos. 8, 106, 277.

East Londoners have been going 'dahn the Roman' for over a hundred and fifty years. Although much of the area around Roman Road has changed beyond recognition since the war, with old terraces replaced by Tower Hamlets tower blocks, the market continues to attract thousands of people. Many are former locals who have been re-housed and who faithfully travel miles to get there, sure of a good deal.

Early on Saturday mornings as far as half a mile away the pavements are full of people walking to Roman Road, becoming an ever denser throng. The market, not easily reached by public transport, is held in the narrowest part of Roman Road. For a quarter of a mile the entire roadway is choked with over 250 stalls, and traffic is diverted. On Saturdays the crowds are so thick and slow moving that it can take an hour just to walk through it.

Although one can buy most everyday things in the market or the shops on either side of the road, nine out of ten market stalls and many of the shops sell clothes and fabrics. Roman Road is famous for its 'cabbages' – not the vegetable, but a huge range of new clothes, seconds and discontinued lines which never reach the shops, and left-over rolls and off-cuts of materials and fabrics. Strictly speaking 'cabbages' are new clothes made out of oddments, but there is much more than this. Roman Road market offers unbeatable value in London for children's clothes, shoes, fashionware, shirts and coats. Moreover there are good quality clothes such as Marks and Spencer or Mothercare seconds, not just the cheap knock-down rubbish one finds so often in markets. The size of the market attracts specialists – a stall of zips and buttons, or pitch No. 124 which sells wigs, displayed on awful heads with peeling gold paint.

There is a strong community spirit and traditional friendliness within the market. Harry da Costa, chairman of the traders' association, runs a lingerie stall which has been in the family for a century; he still serves people who bought from his grandfather! Everyone is on first-name terms. 'The Roman' is more solidly cockney than any other market; it lacks the ethnic variety of Hackney or the Jewish Sunday traditions of Whitechapel. On the corner of Roman Road and Vernon Road is the Poplar Boxing Club, one of East London's most celebrated sporting venues.

Further west along Roman Road towards Bethnal Green is a small daily general market with about a dozen stalls. They used to operate in the road but a new square was created in front of the blocks of flats built next to Morpeth Road in 1961. Like Watney and Chrisp Streets, it is run as a municipal market. No. 77 Roman Road is Capaldi's Ice Cream shop, opened in 1936. Peter Capaldi pioneered the ice cream bicycle and pedalled the streets shouting, 'Peter's ices are good to eat, fresh and sweet, Peter's ices are a treat.'

135

Russell Square, WC1

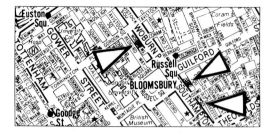

Merchandise: Second-hand and antiquarian books, manuscripts, maps and prints.

Opening times and location: Second week each month: Royal National Hotel, Woburn Place, 10 a.m. to 7 p.m. Sunday, Monday, Tuesday; Russell Hotel, Russell Square, 10.30 a.m. to 7 p.m. Monday, Tuesday, Wednesday; Bonnington Hotel, Southampton Row, 9.30 a.m. to 7 p.m. Monday and Tuesday. Check for details with hotels.

Nearest tube: Russell Square (Piccadilly).

Buses: Nos. 68, 77, 168, 188.

Nearly twenty years ago half a dozen West Country booksellers gathered in Kensington to exchange stock. From this modest overture, a regular book fair became established in London, snowballed, and from 1975 settled in Bloomsbury, in the splendid ballroom of the Imperial Hotel. Old and rare books are now very big business and London is the undisputed centre for British and many foreign dealers.

The once-a-month fair has grown into an enormous and complicated amalgam of venues, mainly in the big hotels around Russell Square. The Provincial Booksellers' Fairs Association organizes the fair in the Russell Hotel on behalf of its subscribers. Two hundred booksellers from every corner of the realm fill the Winter Garden and adjoining rooms with tightly packed rows of shelves lined with thousands of second-hand books. Buyers and sellers clog the narrow gangways and hundreds of quiet, knowledgeable hagglings coalesce into a babbling hum. The Royal National Bookfair is similar though held in the more modern Cambridge Rooms just up the road, which enables buyers to visit both. Dealers' specialisms are remarkable – topography, history, botany, biography, children's books and art books. The monthly *Bookdealer* is crammed with requests for 'pre-1950 books on Abyssinia', 'antique hand-coloured prints of dragonflies', '1910 cricket memoirs' . . . Many displays betray the fusty, undiscovered charm of small country-town bookshops. As you thumb the pages of an eyecatching volume, imagine yourself in the narrow streets of Faversham, Bath, Harrogate, Stamford or Bury St Edmunds. The prices pencilled inside will bring you down to earth. The second-hand trade has never been stronger, nor the demand for dealing space.

Other fairs feed on the dealers and sellers already in town. The Antiquarian Map and Print Fair in the Derby Suite of the Bonnington Hotel claims to be the only monthly map fair in the world – a wonderful place to admire an amazing collection, if not to buy. Outside Bloomsbury, St Olave's Parish Hall, Mark Lane, hosts a small regular market. Several entrepreneurs organize fairs in posh West End venues, the Café Royal or the Park Lane Hotel. These often require admission by expensive brochure, discouraging the casual public, advertised only within the trade. Oddly, Farringdon Road book market, though tiny and less benign, is far better known to private collectors, and is the place to go for unexpected bargains. Long may it continue. Nevertheless, salubrious Russell Square will delight the dedicated bookworm.

Westmoreland Road, SE17

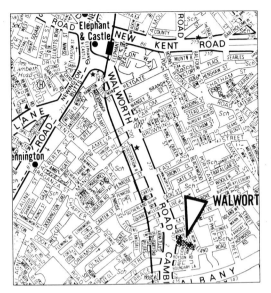

Merchandise: Antiques, furniture and junk on Sunday. Small general market weekdays.

Opening times: 8.30 a.m. to 12.30 p.m. Sunday; 9 a.m. to 4 p.m. Tuesday to Saturday.

Location: Westmoreland Road, from Walworth Road to Queen's Row.

Nearest tube: Elephant and Castle, Kennington (Northern, Bakerloo).

Buses: Nos. 12, 35, 40, 45, 68, 171, 176, 184 (Walworth Road).

Westmoreland Road lives very much in the shadow of East Street market. During the week the small general market suffers from the competition and only a handful of stalls bother to set up. Westmoreland Road then is as quiet and empty as East Street is lively and crowded.

On Sunday, when separate licences are required, it is different. Westmoreland Road has become increasingly specialized as a Sunday market for second-hand furniture, semi-antiques, bric-à-brac and junk. There are usually about fifty stalls lining both sides of the street displaying all sorts of unwanted paraphernalia and curiosities. As it is relatively unknown it is still a place for real bargains, a brass bedstead, an Edwardian lamp-

shade, a Victorian paperweight or an early edition of *Barnaby Rudge*. In Dickens's youth Walworth was still half out in the country, an odd collection of rundown suburban shacks and market gardens.

The back part of Walworth is a straggling miserable place enough, even in these days; thirty-five years ago the greater portion of it was little better than a dreary waste, inhabited by a few scattered people of most questionable character, whose poverty prevented their living in any better neighbourhood, or whose pursuits and mode of life rendered its solitude particularly desirable. (*Sketches by Boz.*)

The eccentric Wemmick in *Great Expectations* lived in his 'castle' in Walworth, a small wooden cottage where everything was on a miniature scale. Walworth shanty town subsequently became a slum with chronic overcrowding and poverty, which is when the market in Westmoreland Road began.

On weekdays the street has little to recommend it. Arment's eel and pie restaurant is a basic affair with formica tables and steamed-up windows. The tropical fish shop no doubt supplies goldfish by the shoal to the tenants of the adjacent fourteen-storey housing estate where cats and dogs must have a hard time. The Bricklayers Arms on the corner with Queen's Row is pleasant enough, but real Walworth enthusiasts might prefer the Duke of Sutherland in Lorrimore Road on the other side of Walworth Road, a back-street local with fine old beer-engines.

Part Four

Billingsgate, E14 (formerly EC3)

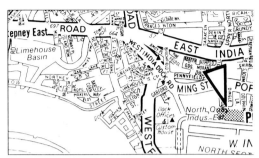

Above New Market. *Below* Old Market

Merchandise: Fish, fresh and smoked, freshwater and sea, shellfish.

Opening times: 5.30 a.m. to 10 a.m. Tuesday to Saturday.

Location: New market, north quay of West India Dock, Isle of Dogs. Old market, south side of Lower Thames Street west of Custom House.

Nearest railway station: For new market – West India Quay (Docklands Light Railway).

Nearest tube: For Old market – Monument (District, Circle).

Buses: Nos. 5, 15, 40, 106, 277, N95 (East India Dock Road), nos. 8A, 10, 15, 21, 35, 40, 43, 44, 47, 48 (Monument).

On Saturday, 16 January 1982 nine hundred years of trading ended at old Billingsgate market and on the following Tuesday a new fish market opened on the Isle of Dogs. It was a nostalgic day for all those who knew the market or were involved in the fish industry, and a sad event in the history of London.

In comparison with the old market the new Billingsgate is an uninspiring place – a thirteen-acre site on the north quay of the West India Dock. Operations are centred round Shed No. 36, a vast modern warehouse converted into a market hall and huge freezing rooms for storing unsold fish. Outside there are great expanses of tarmac for lorry parking. It is a monotonous and grey landscape which seems to have rubbed off on the people who work there, for the market has nothing like the spectacle or hubbub of the old Billingsgate.

Billingsgate is synonymous with fish and has no rival in Britain. Of all London's markets old Billingsgate was regarded with the greatest affection. Its removal attracted unexpected publicity, not as much perhaps as Covent Garden did, but surprising in view of the lack of community involvement in the development plans.

The tradition of fish at Billingsgate stretches back to Saxon times. The name probably derives from a Saxon called Beling who owned the wharves just east of the old London Bridge (the bridgehead has recently been discovered). Less probable is the fanciful but oft quoted legend of an ancient king of the Britons named Belin who, 400 years before Christ, built a commemorative gate at this landing point; unlikely, as London didn't exist then! The Romans constructed a wharf at Billingsgate and a gateway in their river wall. Although the gate was washed away, Billingsgate in Saxon times was one of the City's main quays. Ethelred the Unready collected tolls on vessels arriving at 'Blynesgate' and a customs house was erected.

In 1279 it was decreed that all ships had to be moored overnight at either Queenshythe above London Bridge or Billingsgate. By now Billingsgate had become a major wholesale market, owned and run by the City authorities, for fish, coal, and corn,

(*overleaf*) Smithfield

all of which arrived in large quantities by boat. Fish was the staple diet of Londoners in the Middle Ages partly because it was cheap and plentiful and partly because meat-eating was forbidden on many days by the Catholic Church; it was possible to observe 150 fish days per year. One of the main retail fish markets was in Friday Street, EC4. By 1559 Billingsgate had become restricted to fish, and a Royal Charter in 1699 gave Billingsgate monopolistic rights as London's fish market.

by the City Corporation. The new Shadwell fish market was not a success. Some thought was given in 1908 to moving Billingsgate there; but a year later the Shadwell market was closed.

Victorian Billingsgate was London's noisiest market. Traders and salesman shouted each other down as they competed for customers, the porters bellowed abuse and anecdotes, and steel-rimmed carts and barrows added to the din. Since medieval times Billingsgate has been renowned for its foul

Tegg's famous fishwives, foul-mouthed and thick-skinned (G.L.C.)

Just one petrol-driven vehicle among a sea of horses; hard to believe this was 1937 (Museum of London)

Between 1848 and 1852 the old jetties were filled in and the market sheds rebuilt by James Bunning, City architect, who had designed the Coal Exchange over the road. In 1874 the market was enlarged by Bunning's successor, Horace Jones, at a cost of £300,000. Encouraged by the general acclaim for his new Smithfield market, Jones used a pleasant combination of cast iron, brick and Portland stone, giving the market an imposing façade to the waterfront and to the street. Cavernous basements were built beneath the market hall for storage, into which refrigerators were installed in the 1880s. The new buildings gave Billingsgate a new lease of life and greatly improved efficiency. It was just in time; in 1885 a rival private market was opened down river at Shadwell even though the enabling Act of 1882 had been opposed

language, a synonym for profane and bawdy talk. Shakespeare recognized this: '... as bad a tongue, if it be set on, as any oyster-wife at Billingsgate' (*King Lear*). Nevertheless Mayhew was entranced by the market: 'In the darkness of the shed the white bellies of the turbots, strung up bow-fashion, shine like mother-of-pearl, while the lobsters, lying upon them, look intensely scarlet from the contrast.' Most of the fish still arrived by boat, even with the advent of the railways, and the quays thronged with sailors, dockers and fishwives.

Fish continued to come by boat well into this century, not on the trawlers but on larger feeder boats delivering 400 tons of fish per day. The last fish boats sailed up the Thames in the late 1940s. Thereafter the railways took over – freight trains from Hull, Grimsby, Fleetwood and Aberdeen. Railway wagons were carried on trailers down from King's Cross and packed into the yard beside the market. Lorries replaced rail in the late 1960s and at the same time the plans for turning Upper and Lower Thames Street into an urban motorway were pushed forward. In their obsession with

creating a southern bypass for the City, the Corporation killed any chance of Billingsgate surviving on its original site. The haddock market on the north side of the street was demolished and the road widened. Lower Thames Street in the 1970s became a nightmare for the market, dangerous to cross, unpleasant to work beside, disruptive to the market's operations. The City Corporation argued that Billingsgate was equally obstructive to their road scheme. They wanted to pull it down and be rid of the nuisance. The idea of building a new road next to the river (as in Paris) or not building a road at all was never seriously considered. Plans for redeveloping the market on an adjacent site were abandoned; offices were more lucrative.

Meanwhile the Victorian buildings remained unimproved. The market hall was dark, cold and draughty, the floor wet and slippery. Each day any unsold fish had to be taken down to the basement coldstore with its archaic ammonia freezers and brought up again on slow hydraulic lifts before the next day's trading. The lorry yard was ill-suited to juggernauts which frequently blocked half the

Harold Vines, Dave Marshall and Bill Rush; faces from old Billingsgate (Museum of London)

width of the road outside the market during unloading or 'unshoring' in the early hours. Facilities for workers and customers were rudimentary. Worst of all, the volume of fish sold dwindled steadily.

Before the market closed it was increasingly hemmed in as an unwanted misfit. This part of the City had once been a commercial and trading area. The fish merchants in Lovat Lane and Fish Street Hill closed in the 1970s; the old man who made the traditional porters' black leather and cork 'bobbin-hats', padded for carrying baskets of fish, disappeared with them. The pubs which used to open early in the morning stopped doing so. They were making enough out of lunchtime businessmen; the fishy smells, dirty clothes and foul language of the market no longer suited their image.

In its new surroundings the market continues to operate along similar lines to the old Billingsgate. It remains a sample market; the bulk of the fish stays on the lorry. Unshoring of sample boxes begins at 5 a.m. and trading starts at 5.30 a.m. Theoretically this carries on until 3 p.m. but in practice the buyers are gone by 10 and telephone dealing lasts only until lunch. Two hundred tons of fish pass through the market every morning, half the pre-war volume. The variety of fish is fantastic, from the ordinary

cod and herring, packed in ice, to bizarre marine monsters. Not all the fish are dead: there are huge crates brimming with crabs, tubs of whelks and winkles, Scottish and Canadian lobsters, oysters snuggled in seaweed to keep them happy, and aluminium barrels seething with eels. The crabs and whelks are cooked on site and eels bloodily chopped into segments for jellying. The Billingsgate merchants pride themselves on being able to obtain any fish, however unusual, required by a customer – shark, red snapper, flying fish, octopus or sting-ray. Billingsgate is crucial for most of Britain's fishing ports and big fleets, very few of which can dispose of all their catch locally or to fish-finger factories. The merchants have kept the old system of tolls, paid on incoming fish, at about five pence per cwt. It is old fashioned but fair, and keeps the rents lower.

Most of the ninety merchants in the old market moved to the Isle of Dogs. A few who were near retirement called it a day, unable to face the upheaval after a life in familiar surroundings. Some smaller dealers merged.

Nearly all the 170 porters also moved, including Manny Abrahams who still wears his father's old basin hat. Several veterans retired which allowed some of the waiting 'stand-boys', apprentices to the salesmen, to get their porter's badges. The move was bad for the 'scats', tramps who at old Billingsgate had picked up work on the side, carrying ice or acting as pushers for heavy barrows being pulled up Monument Street. Porters are paid piece-rate by the merchants who levy porterage whether the customers use the porters or not. Forklift trucks mean that fewer porters are needed, especially casual porters 'on the stones', but the union is regulating numbers by natural wastage. The traditional image of the porter with a white coat carrying boxes of fish on his leather hat across slippery cobbles is a fading memory. Only the wellies and waders survive.

The special market police came too. Theft and pilfering had been widespread in the old market and virtually impossible to control. Some of the victims preferred to turn a blind eye, probably because they were involved in the game themselves. Security should be easier now.

The market superintendent (with the paradoxical name of Butcher) hopes that the new site will reverse the trend of the seventies and attract more trade. The layout is more convenient, the location less so. Although many workers live out east, the Isle of Dogs is badly served by public transport. Worse still, West End buyers have to struggle three miles back into London with the morning traffic. David Butcher believes that a computer fed with the data relevant to the best location in London for a fish market would choose the City, perhaps even the old Billingsgate! The superintendent was in charge of Leadenhall as well as Billingsgate; the link has now been broken.

The £7½ million bill for moving the market was to have been financed by redevelopment of the old

The last morning at old Billingsgate, bobbin-hats worn to the end.

site. Heseltine's decision to list the buildings put a spanner in the City's works. S.A.V.E. and Richard Rogers, of Beaubourg and Coin Street fame, produced a scheme for shops, offices, flats and a riverside walk. Close to the Monument and the Tower, it could become a tourist attraction, though not on the scale of Covent Garden. The underground vaults, frosty catacombs with fairyland stalactites of ice crystals, would be a unique spectacle, 'the suspended breath of generations of porters' oaths'. The London Commodity Exchange, who deal in paper transactions of cocoa, coffee, rubber, sugar, wool and petroleum, are also interested.

Restoration may stop the last piece of the concrete jigsaw of Lower Thames Street, but the fish which gave the area its character have gone for ever. The bricks, tiles, cobbles and timber of old Billingsgate are impregnated with centuries of fish oil. The smell lingered for a while, but no more on a warm summer morning does the rich crude tang of fish drift up the alleys and lanes towards East Cheap and the financial palaces of Lombard Street. Fish Street Hill and Fishmongers' Hall by London Bridge are left as quaint reminders, just as so many City street names politely and irrelevantly recall the past.

On that last cold Saturday morning as dawn broke outside old Billingsgate joking porters lined up for final cups of tea in the lorry park. Some well-known mugs were laced with generous nips of scotch, kept handy under the counter, to make 'wazzers', as they are known at Smithfield. 'Well, I've 'ad me last piss against the Thames wall,' laughed one, 'and 'tis a bloody shame, so give us a drop of the medicine.' One hopes for the sake of the fish trade that new Billingsgate does not fail. It was moved in the name of progress by the authorities who know best, and with it disappeared a little chunk of old London.

Borough, SE1

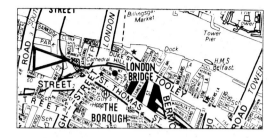

Merchandise: Vegetables, fruit and flowers.

Opening times: 5.30 a.m. to 1 p.m. Monday to Saturday.

Location: West side of Borough High Street bounded by Bedale Street, Stoney Street and Winchester Walk.

Nearest tube: London Bridge (Northern).

Buses: Nos. 8A, 10, 17, 21, 35, 40, 43, 44, 47, 48, 70, 133, 501, N47, N89 (Borough High Street).

Southwark, literally the southern bulwark or fortification of London Bridge, has been a settlement since Roman times. As the earliest outpost or suburb of London it was known in the Middle Ages as the Borough. Borough High Street was the southern approach to London Bridge, the road from the south-east and Europe. Here late travellers would spend the night in one of the inns or taverns when the great gates on the bridge were closed at sundown, and Chaucer's pilgrims would gather before their trek to Canterbury.

The Borough was also a natural location for the exchange of goods. Southwark Fair was one of the main medieval pedlars' and tinkers' markets bringing European luxuries to London's doorstep. Kent was aptly named the Garden of England before the Fens were drained, and supplied London with most of its fruit and vegetables. Borough was the best place for the Kent farmers to sell their produce to City greengrocers. We know that the market was held originally on London Bridge itself which supported houses and shops. In 1276 the market was moved into Borough High Street, known then as the King's Highway; the bridge masters bemoaned the loss of tolls. Edward VI granted a charter for the City Corporation to run the market.

Borough market and Southwark Fair attracted all kinds of diversions. Bear Gardens, off Bankside, was popular for its bear-baiting, where packs of dogs were set on tethered bears. Both Pepys and Evelyn witnessed bear fights here and found them 'a barbarous and nasty pleasure'. When brothels were banned from the City the stews at Southwark became a convenient alternative, with ferries plying across the river. Miscreants were thrown into the jail in Clink Street, next to the Bishop of Winchester's Palace.

By 1754 the volume of traffic and cattle in Borough High Street had become so bad that the fruit and vegetable market could no longer function properly and the Corporation abandoned it. On 25 March 1756 the old market closed and by the same Act of Parliament a new market was established close by on ground known as the Triangle. The rights to hold the market were vested in the Churchwardens, Overseers and Inhabitants of the Parish of St Saviour, Southwark, under the control of 120 commissioners. The market was to remain for ever an estate for the use and benefit of the Parish, with profits applied to the diminution of parochial rates. No one could hold a rival market within 1,000 yards, which is still strictly observed today.

Borough market went from strength to strength. It easily shrugged off competition from St George's market, opened by James Hedger near Elephant and Castle in 1789, which within fifty years was in a lamentable state of neglect. When the South East Railway to Cannon Street and Charing Cross was constructed in 1862 Borough market was enlarged. In 1932 the seventeenth-century houses of Three Crown Square were demolished and, at a cost of £50,000, the Triangle was extended to give direct access on to Borough High Street with new offices over the frontage. The market stands were further increased in 1962 and Stoney Street was widened.

The Trustees now control a four-acre site. The main part, the Inner Market, comprises three acres, bounded by the High Street, Bedale Street (known until 1800 as Foul Lane), Winchester Street and Stoney Street (once noted for its paving). Compared with Covent Garden or Spitalfields,

Borough is small. However, bigger does not mean better; for vegetables and friendly attentive service Borough has no rival.

Within the Inner Market sixty-four wholesale merchants rent stands on a weekly basis. Produce arrives at night, by lorry these days. William and Edward Frisby who worked at the Borough for sixty years recall how fruit and vegetables used to arrive in horse-drawn wagons. Quite often the drivers who were full of ale would be fast asleep, but their horses always remembered the route and brought them safely here. Lorries aren't the same.

The market superintendent employs twelve pitchers who help unload the produce into the tenants' stalls. Pitching takes place any time from 10 p.m. onwards reaching a peak at 3 a.m. Priority is given to the growers' stands, which since 1829 have been demarcated for growers to expose and sell their wares. The growers are exempt from the market tolls collected on top of rents. The market police, known at Borough as 'beadles', assess the tolls, checking each incoming lorry, as well as watching out for pilfering. Cliff Tate, chief beadle, is a burly man with a booming drillground voice. He and his assistants know everyone in the market. Theft is minimal compared with larger wholesale markets.

Trading starts at 5.30 a.m. and is busiest between 6 and 9 a.m., especially on Tuesday, Thursday, Friday and Saturday. Every tenant has his particular speciality: Bourne and Wildenberg deal in potatoes, home-grown and imported from Egypt and the Canaries – one dealer visits Cornwall for two weeks each year to buy up the new potato crop; Sugarman's large stand in the Jubilee section next to Winchester Street specializes in fruit, varying with the seasons – Cyprus grapes, Israeli oranges, South African grapefruit, Australian peaches, English strawberries, Canadian apples and Algerian tangerines. Long-established firms like Arnold, Stubbins and Newton, Webbs, or Terry the mushroom king, deal in traditional English vegetables. Lucas and Hinton and Woolgar have banana-ripening rooms in the outer market. Some bananas are sold green for the West Indian markets.

Many stands put on a lavish display to attract buyers who walk round comparing and negotiating prices. Most buyers are small greengrocers, street traders or costermongers, often scorned at the larger markets but welcomed at Borough. Each tenant employs porters to load the buyers' vans and carts. Forklift trucks are widely used although the traditional barrow still comes in handy. The old custom of carrying baskets on the head has disappeared. Borough market-hands used to compete in the annual basket-carrying races at Crystal Palace.

The market employs about 250 people, including porters, pitchers, salesmen, clerks and beadles. The union and the Market Tenants' Association are well organized and, in collaboration with the Trustees, have improved parking and ramping. Throughput has declined but not drastically. A few years ago Borough appeared to be losing out to the New Covent Garden, but the small scale and obliging service have won some customers back, although Borough cannot compete for fruit. Spare stock is stored overnight in the stands. Substandard deliveries are returned to the sender with a certificate from the Public Health Inspector as proof. Frosted potatoes may be sold cheap for fish and chips.

At Borough a communal spirit prevails. Everybody gets their hands dirty; no one stands around in a three-piece suit watching other people do the work. Most tenants had grandfathers at Borough, some are intermarried, and there is an unpretentious pride and fierce independence in the market. The Trustees serve voluntarily and none lives more than half a mile from the market. Fred Cullen, the superintendent, has spent forty-three years at Borough and has a few years left before retiring. He rejects the recent Government report criticizing the smaller wholesale markets and remains loyally committed to Borough: 'nobody can force us to move, Borough is here to stay'. There seems no reason to doubt him.

Sheltered under the railway arches and in the shadow of Southwark Cathedral, Borough market, with its heady aroma of onions, cabbages, oranges and geraniums, has charm and character. Until the last war the Hop Exchange and thirty hop merchants operated in Southwark Street; before digits took over, Southwark's telephone exchange was HOP. The only hops now to be found are in the beer. Several of the local pubs such as the Wheatsheaf, Southwark Tavern and Market Porter in Stoney Street or the Globe in Bedale Street open from 6.30 a.m. for the salesmen, buyers and porters. Sam Weller in *Pickwick Papers* refreshed himself at one of them with an early lunch of 'two or three pounds of cold beef and a pot or two of porter after the fatigues of the Borough Market'. Dickens, a Kentish man, was familiar with Borough High Street and knew the George at No. 77, famous for its galleried coaching yard. It is one of the few inns in London where he might still feel at home.

New Covent Garden, SW8

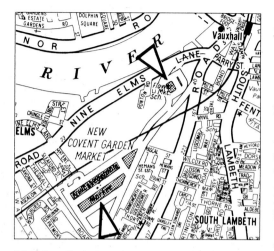

Merchandise: Fruit, vegetables and flowers.

Opening times: 4 a.m. to 11 a.m. Monday to Friday. Saturdays in summer only.

Location: Between Nine Elms Lane and Wandsworth Road.

Nearest tube: Vauxhall (Victoria).

Buses: Nos. 44, 170, N88 (Nine Elms Lane), nos. 77, 77A, N68 (Wandsworth Road).

New Covent Garden is London's biggest and most modern market as well as being the largest horticultural market in the United Kingdom. When the market moved in 1974 from old Covent Garden over three hundred years of tradition were lost, which saddened many people. However the new premises three miles away at Nine Elms have enabled the market to flourish again as the cornerstone for the distribution of fruit, vegetables and flowers in Britain. The new market is custom-built, efficient, inaccessible to casual onlookers, unglamorous – all the things that old Covent Garden was not.

Covent Garden was until the sixteenth century a convent garden belonging to and supplying the Abbey of Westminster. After the Dissolution the three-acre garden passed to the Crown and in 1552 was granted to John Russell, first Earl of Bedford, together with seven acres of land to the north, known to this day as Long Acre. The fourth Earl was keen to develop the land and in 1630 employed

Inigo Jones to design the Piazza, London's first square. The Piazza, which included St Paul's Church on the west side, became a fashionable address for the court and minor aristocracy, but in 1670 William Russell, fifth Earl, was granted a charter by Charles II to hold a market in the Piazza for the sale of horticultural produce.

During the eighteenth century, much to the annoyance of the local residents, the market grew rapidly, matching London's demand for fresh fruit and vegetables to feed an expanding population. Inigo Jones's colonnaded arcades around the Piazza were gradually replaced by more modern buildings and wooden market huts appeared. By 1800 there were 15,000 acres of market gardens within ten miles of Covent Garden. Each night the farmers loaded their carts and set off for market. In season strawberries, ever the Englishman's delight, were carried by hundreds of women who came up from the provinces specially for the work.

Following an Act of Parliament new graceful buildings were erected by Charles Fowler in 1830 in the middle of the Piazza, and added to later in the century. The market was one of London's great institutions, crowded with besmocked countrymen, aproned costers and greengrocers with their carts and barrows, porters struggling under the weight of piles of baskets balanced on their heads, Irish apple-sellers, flower girls and urchins. It fascinated Dickens:

Covent Garden on market morning is wonderful company . . . at sunrise in the spring or summer, when the fragrance of sweet flowers is in the air, overpowering even the unwholesome streams of last night's debauchery, and driving the dusky thrush, whose cage has hung outside a garret window all night long, half mad with joy . . . but one of the worst night sights I know in London is to be found in the children who prowl about this place, and are perpetually making a blunt pattering on the pavement of the Piazza with the rain of their naked feet. (*The Old Curiosity Shop.*)

By the time Eliza Doolittle was 'found' under the porch of St Paul's Church, local market garden produce was being replaced by imported fruit and vegetables brought by steam-ship and railway, and

South side of the old market, 1902, St Paul's church behind. A teeming mass of carts, porters, fruit and vegetables (G.L.C.)

1895, market morning at old Covent Garden. Note the baskets rather than barrows (G.L.C.)

aided by refrigeration. More premises were built and increasingly the trade took over buildings in adjoining streets, eventually occupying about thirty acres. In 1918 the eleventh Duke of Bedford sold the market buildings to a property company and in 1961 the Covent Garden Market Authority was established by Act of Parliament to take over the six-acre central market properties.

The Authority's brief was to examine the future of the market, which housed over 250 traders and 5,000 buyers each day. Tenants were experiencing great difficulties in operating: traffic congestion had become chronic – large lorries had to battle through the West End and then clashed with theatreland traffic in the narrow streets around the market; the buildings were old and unable to adapt to more efficient handling methods (right up to the end the

Part Four Wholesale Markets

Women pea-shellers, 1930 (Guildhall Library)

Outside the west portico of St Paul's, 1930 (G.L.C.)

market relied on hand-barrows and head-carrying by porters); adjacent warehouses were insecure and open to theft; and local residents suffered intolerable noise and dirt.

Redevelopment on the old site was quickly rejected. The decision to move was made in 1966, and in 1971, when public spending restrictions were lifted, construction started at Nine Elms. Consultants had studied many sites in London, and in fact recommended a suburban location at Romford. The traders chose Vauxhall, acutely aware that 20 per cent of their custom was from the West End and that this would be lost to other markets such as Borough or Spitalfields if they moved east.

The move was made on 12 November 1974 with surprisingly little bother. It left a huge vacuum in Covent Garden and a gigantic headache for the planners, community groups and politicians – first a crisis of dereliction and conservation, later a problem of excess affluence and competition for space.

Enormous thought went into the new buildings at Nine Elms. The sixty-eight-acre site, though dissected by the Waterloo railway line, was generous and gave ample scope to build a hygienic and efficient food-handling depot.

The main vehicle entrances are from Nine Elms Lane, reminiscent of ferryport control points or motorway toll stations. Vehicles pay on entry, which raises nearly £½ million per year for the Market Authority. The railway separates the fruit and vegetable market from the flower market but tunnels connect all parts. Vast areas are given over to vehicle circulation, unloading and parking; 2,000 lorries and 1,000 cars can be accommodated at any one time.

The fruit and vegetable market occupies two identical parallel buildings both 1,200 feet long and 155 feet wide. The 170-foot gap is bridged by two elevated links which contain pubs, cafés, banks and shops. Buyers' walks run longitudinally down the centre of both buildings. Each trader has a frontage on to the buyers' walk for display and rear servicing to the outside for delivery and loading. Everything is carried by forklift and the width of each bay is based on the most economic pallet-stacking configuration. In the lorry parks goods are transferred to forklifts under cover. Most produce goes through the tenants' stands though some sample selling occurs with goods remaining on lorries.

The 120 tenants pay rent and service charge according to the amount of space they occupy (there are no tolls). Size varies, from major importing and distributing groups, filling dozens of stands, to single-man specialists. Some require large stores for ripening bananas and citrus fruit. Most operate on commission, acting as agents for growers and overseas suppliers, getting the best price and taking their cut, usually 6 to 10 per cent on fruit and veg., 10 to 15 per cent on flowers. The growers' pavilion is sited at the eastern end of the main building with forty covered stands specifically allocated to Home Counties farmers who can park and sell from their own vehicles. Although it accounts for only 1 per cent of the trade, and is less important than it used to be in old Covent Garden, the growers provide a useful barometer for buyers of fresh English fruit and vegetables.

Buyers also vary: retailing greengrocers, hoteliers and caterers come from all over London, especially the south and west but, more significantly, the market attracts primary and secondary wholesalers from all over Great Britain who in turn supply markets and retailers in the provinces. Prices are set at Covent Garden which influence the whole country. Such is the size of the market that, like Billingsgate for fish, it acts as a clearing house for unsold local surplus anywhere in the U.K. (hence the explanation for Cornish potatoes on sale in Truro market which have been to Covent Garden!). Supermarkets tend to have their own direct suppliers, but come to Covent Garden to top up, often for exotic fruit.

Covent Garden receives produce from about seventy countries, and therefore knows no season. There are strawberries in July and January, either from Kent or Egypt; only the price is different. The English palate has become more adventurous, perhaps because of foreign holidays, perhaps because of Commonwealth immigrants.

Deliveries arrive from 11 p.m. onwards and buying starts at 4 a.m. In a modern market this might seem unnecessary, but it suits the London buyer who wants fresh produce in his shop by 9 a.m. Thursday and Friday are always busy, Monday and Tuesday less so, except at Christmas and Easter.

The flower market is north of the railway, next to the high Market Towers office block. Exactly square, it consists of a 70,000-square-foot open market hall, spanned by a remarkable translucent glass-reinforced polyester roof moulded into inverted pyramids. Natural light is augmented by colour-corrective strips, and all incoming air through the automatic doors is filtered and temperature kept constant at 14 °C all year. During most months the air has to be cooled rather than heated. The traders' stands are divided by honey-combed aluminium partitions.

The ninety traders and numerous buyers are both big and small, from Interflora to the Friday flower man on a street corner. The Market Authority employs ten porters to unload while the tenants have their own porters for carrying out. Unlike the fruit and vegetable market there are no forklifts, only barrows. New Covent Garden is convenient for Heathrow, and plants and flowers arrive from twenty countries, the U.S.A., Holland,

Australia, Singapore and South America supplying the craze for exotic tropical houseplants – yuccas, cheese and rubber plants. In December Christmas trees swell the evergreen ranks, while in the week before Mothering Sunday the market hall is ablaze with colour and heady with scent. Around the side are small stalls for sundriesmen selling pots, ribbons, wire, bags and even plastic flowers. Offices and cafés overlook the hall. The market bars open at 5 a.m., but not, alas, the older pubs outside like the Surprise in Wandsworth Road.

The Market Authority, a Government body reporting to the Ministry of Agriculture, employs only seventy people. Thirty-six of these are beadles who police traffic and theft. Pilfering is difficult to prevent in such a huge market; even forklift trucks have disappeared. Nevertheless theft represents less than 1 per cent of throughput. Rubbish disposal, a massive task with everything arriving in boxes, and building maintenance are subcontracted. The market itself employs over 3,000 people of whom

650 are porters working piece-rate for the tenants. The T.G.W.U. controls the porters' licences and supervised the loss of 150 porters when the market moved to Nine Elms.

Without tolls there is no direct check on through-put but tenants submit annual returns: in 1973 turnover was worth £80 million; in 1981 this had risen to £220 million. Fruit and vegetables, worth £183 million, were 9 per cent up on 1980; flowers at £36 million were 17 per cent up. The Market Authority's profits repay the £43 million borrowed to build the market, although the Government intends selling Market Towers to speed this up.

Trade lost when the old market was choked by congestion in the 1960s has returned. But what of the future? The geometry of the site limits room for growth. While this is not a problem in the fruit and vegetable market where 10 per cent of space is unlet, the flower market is bursting at the seams. Its shape allows no easy expansion. There is a feeling that the market should attract more supermarket buyers (25 per cent of retail sales do not go through

markets). To change this, quality control must be improved and poor or badly graded fruit returned to the grower. Quality control requires well-trained inspection when goods arrive, but how many senior personnel want to be on duty at four o'clock every morning? Perhaps in time two markets will emerge, one early morning market for small greengrocers and one during office hours for large wholesalers and supermarket buyers.

New Covent Garden is bigger than all the other wholesale horticultural markets in London put together, but in terms of character it doesn't compare. Nine Elms is a barren wasteland sur-rounded by railway sidings, Battersea Power Station, new warehouses and arterial roads. Even Wilcox Road market off Wandsworth Road is extinct. Visitors to New Covent Garden tend to be from trade delegations rather than sightseers. Perhaps in a hundred and fifty years we will regard the present buildings with the same affection as Fowler's market hall, carefully preserved in old Covent Garden. Fifteen years is too soon to judge.

Smithfield, EC1

Merchandise: Meat, poultry and game.

Opening times: 5 a.m. to 9 a.m. Monday to Friday.

Location: Between West Smithfield and Charterhouse Street.

Nearest tube: Farringdon, Barbican (Circle, Metropolitan), Chancery Lane (Central).

Buses: Nos. 4, 279A (Aldersgate Street), nos. 17, 63, 221, 259, N21, N83, N93, N96 (Farringdon Road), nos. 8, 22, 25, 501, N89, N95, N98 (Holborn Viaduct), nos. 277, 279 (St John Street).

The London Central Markets, more commonly known as Smithfield, is the oldest and largest wholesale meat market in Europe, and most people in Britain will have heard of it. With Billingsgate fish market finally gone to docklands, Smithfield is the last of the great medieval markets on its original site, with a history stretching back a thousand years.

Once a 'smooth field' in the shadow of the old Roman city walls, Smithfield began in late Saxon times as the site for a weekly livestock and cattle market. It was described in 1174 as 'a smooth field where every Friday there is a celebrated rendezvous of fine horses to be sold, and in another quarter are placed vendibles of the peasant, swine with their deep flanks, and cows and oxen of immense bulk'.

The open land was also used for jousting, football and archery, and for three days in August for the great Bartholomew Fair which developed from a medieval cloth fair into one of London's most riotous carnivals and public holidays. During the sixteenth century the area around the cattle market became densely built up with streets and houses, one of London's earliest suburbs. At the bottom end of St John Street were the Smithfield bars, wooden barriers across the road where tolls and dues were levied and vagabonds turned away from the City.

In 1614 the market was paved and drained for the first time and considerably extended up towards the Charterhouse. A formal Royal Charter was declared in 1638 even though tolls had been collected since the 1300s. London's population continued to grow rapidly and the market was now operating most days a week. By 1725 London was consuming 60,000 cattle, 70,000 sheep and 240,000 pigs each year. Animals were driven enormous distances from all over the country to Smithfield market, cattle from Scotland and Wales, sheep from Lincoln and the West Country, geese and turkeys from Suffolk and Norfolk, often wearing little cloth shoes to protect their feet.

This was the age of the drover and his roads; St John Street was the main approach to the market. Huge droves of cattle would congregate at Islington for fattening in the meadows and pastures. The country drovers handed over the herds to the London drovers who then guided the great streams of animals down the winding length of St John Street into the market. Animals were slaughtered in appalling conditions in Smithfield and Newgate, and dead meat sold in the old medieval Shambles market in Newgate Street. The agricultural revolution in the eighteenth century and its introduction of winter fodder crops enabled animals to be fattened for slaughter and Smithfield market to operate all year round.

By 1800 Smithfield was reaching saturation point, the result of an expanding population, increased meat-eating and a confined site. Public indignation at the continuation of the cattle market mounted; the dung, flies and danger to pedestrians were becoming intolerable. Clearly the heart of an ever-spreading London was no place for livestock; but despite growing pressure the City Corporation who owned the market and collected the dues were reluctant to act. Eventually a Royal Commission was set up and in 1852 the Smithfield Removal Act was passed, forcing the City authorities to relocate the market. A new open site was found north of

Shepherd's view of Smithfield from the bars in St John Street, 1820 (Museum of London)

Islington, called Copenhagen Fields, and here in 1855 the Caledonian cattle market was opened.

No sooner had the cattle market left than the railway arrived in Smithfield; the Metropolitan line was opened in 1863 and terminated at Farringdon station. The Shambles market was closed and on the empty land at Smithfield a new dead meat market was erected by the City Corporation; this survives today. The Metropolitan railway effectively linked Smithfield to every corner of Britain and was the chief raison d'être behind the brilliant design. With the railway already underground the market was built on two levels – a basement for unloading meat arriving by train and the main market hall above with street-level access for the buyers' carts. Steam-powered lifts raised the meat from the sidings into the market.

The building is a masterpiece of functional and aesthetic design. Horace Jones's architecture shows the influence of Paxton's Crystal Palace and is remarkable for its elaborate cast-iron roof and fine decoration. Four octagonal pavilion towers stand proudly at each corner, while the 630-foot length is relieved by a central arcade, the Grand Avenue, with elliptical arched roof and impressive entrances guarded by Britannia-like statues and fiery dragons. Access into the market, which is 240 feet wide, is by huge intricate cast-iron gates. Viewed through these gates the main thoroughfare of the market is like a cathedral nave, such is the scale and airiness of the place. Either side of the central aisle are the sellers' stalls, each with their overhead rails festooned with meat hooks. The use of open ironwork and louvres was Horace Jones's masterstroke, letting in light and air but shutting out the sun. The ventilation keeps the hanging meat fresh and cool even on the hottest days.

Opened in 1868 with an extravagant back-slapping ceremony, the market proved an immediate success. A new poultry market was built

Edwardian Smithfield, before the lorries, the new poultry market and the plastic canopies (Museum of London)

next to the meat market in 1873, and in 1879 a general market was added at the Farringdon Road end, supposedly to house the defunct Fleet and Farringdon vegetable markets, but soon to be devoted to meat and poultry. In 1958 the poultry market was burnt down and rebuilt to a modern design, but apart from the addition of unattractive canopies to the outside the other building remains unchanged. The vast underground sidings closed in the early 1960s when, after the Beeching axe, deliveries ceased arriving by rail. In 1970 this

cavern was converted into a car park, and now all meat goes in and out of the market at street level. The Victorians would not believe our stupidity.

Unlike other wholesale markets, Smithfield is not a sample market; everything sold is unloaded, carried into the market, displayed, purchased and carried out again. At Billingsgate and New Covent Garden lorries act as warehouses – a buyer will examine a sample box and purchase the lorryload.

Unloading begins at midnight. Huge forty-foot container lorries are now the norm, coming from

Scotland, Eire and Europe. Imports from Argentina and the old Commonwealth into London docks, so important before the war, have now dwindled to only about one fifth of the meat sold at Smithfield and this rarely arrives by sea at London. During the course of one night a piece of meat is handled by several men, each with their own clearly demarcated jobs. First there are 'pullers-back' who drag the carcasses to the tailboard of the lorries, from where pitchers carry the meat on to the hooks inside the market. Nearly all the meat is still carried by hand. Some pitchers go at a half-run to the stalls, minimizing the time with weight on their backs. This is the 'Smithfield Shuffle'; cursed be anyone in the way. Long sides of beef are carried by two pitchers.

At the stalls humpers and shopmen weigh, mark and arrange the meat for display. By 4 a.m. the market is full, a fine sight with row upon row of pigs, lambs and bullocks, and in the poultry market chickens, turkeys, and some geese and rabbits.

Trading begins at 5 a.m., with buyers inspecting the meat and striking deals with the stall tenants.

Many tenants sell meat on commission, so it is in their interest to maximize their rake-off. No prices are displayed until the end of the day, but the tradition of merchants' integrity survives – the word is the bond. Cutting the carcass into manageable portions and primary joints is particularly important and highly skilled. No part of the animal is wasted; huge bins brimming with hearts or livers and carefully folded strips of suet are bought by offal merchants, the piles of severed heads go for brawn. Smithfield is no place for the squeamish.

In the meat market buyers are obliged to use porters to carry their purchases to waiting vans and lorries. Big buyers employ their own porters but others have to use the freelance 'bummarees', who charge per piece carried, cash. This is one of the most sought-after jobs in the market with the highest rewards, and numbers are controlled by licence. In the poultry market buyers can carry out and, though strictly speaking wholesale, it is more accessible to the adventurous shopper seeking a pre-Christmas turkey. Labour costs account for 4 per

cent of the eventual retail price of the meat.

By 8 a.m. most of the business is done and the remaining meat is then taken by barrow to vans, coldstores or nearby butchers. By midday the market is clear, leaving the street cleaners to hose down the bloody pavements. Before long the giant lorries arrive for the following night's market.

The last thirty years have seen tremendous changes in the meat trade. Smithfield has lost out to suburban wholesale depots and supermarket chains with their own abattoirs and meat-processing factories. Central London is increasingly tiresome for Home Counties buyers to reach, and there are those who criticize the market for its antiquated methods, lack of hygiene and high labour charges. The weight of meat handled annually has dwindled, reinforced by the trend to receive pre-boned joints. Since 1985 the volume seems to have stabilized, settling at a new level as the wholesale supplier to inner London butchers, caterers and the hotel and restaurant trade. Inevitably the market now needs to be a smaller, more compact affair. While Christmas remains hectic, at other times the 'village' and former general market at the Farringdon end are very quiet. Many stalls do not open on Fridays.

In 1984 the City Corporation set up a Working Party to assess the future, and to examine options of closure, relocation and refurbishment. The first two were rejected – Smithfield serves a vital function and remains convenient for the West End trade. Local traffic problems have largely solved themselves. The debate has hinged on the extent of refurbishment and the willingness of the unions to cooperate in rationalization and mechanization. Deadlines have been deferred and extended. Currently, the Corporation plans to spend £15 million renovating the main meat and poultry markets, disposing of the buildings to the west. New ventilation and temperature controls, stainless-steel floors, mezzanine ancillary offices, cold-storage facilities and sanitary accommodation are planned, to equip Smithfield for well into the next century.

The market is crucial to the survival of Smithfield as an identifiable area. Already, prestige City offices are pouncing on empty warehouses; chic restaurants are replacing the bacon-curers, offal-merchants and greasy-spoon cafés which once lined the side streets. Plush carpets and pin-stripes now flood the Bishop's Finger in West Smithfield and the Fox and Anchor in Charterhouse Street (renowned for its gargantuan breakfasts), replacing lino and bloodstained white coats. Covent Garden lost its cabbage leaves and wooden pallets to beauty clinics and health-food shops. Meat has been Smithfield's trade for centuries; Cowcross Street and Charterhouse Street have spelt (and smelt) meat. It is one of London's great traditions; long may it live.

Spitalfields, E1

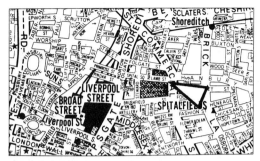

Merchandise: Fruit, vegetables and flowers.

Opening times: 4.30 a.m. to 2.30 p.m. Monday to Saturday.

Location: West side of Commercial Street between Folgate Street and Brushfield Street.

Nearest tube: Liverpool Street (Central, Metropolitan, Circle).

Buses: No. 67 (Commercial Street), nos. 5, 6, 8, 22, 35, 47, 48, 78, 149, 243, N11, N83 (Bishopsgate).

Spitalfields is the largest horticultural wholesale market north of the river, with twelve acres of land and buildings. It may lack the old-world charm of Borough or medieval Smithfield but it is a vital cog in the supply of fruit and vegetables to Londoners. Now its days are numbered; in 1991 it will move to Temple Mills, leaving Spitalfields to the booming City Legoland.

The name derives from the priory and hospital of St Mary, founded in 1197 by Walter and Rosia Brunus on the site of the present-day market. The 'spital' was run by Augustinians and lay help, providing 180 beds for mental patients and relief for London's poor. After the Dissolution the spital fields were sold, developed and settled by Protestant refugees, mainly Huguenots who were renowned for their skill in silkweaving. In 1682 one of the more enterprising silk-throwers, John Balch, was granted a charter to hold a market on Thursdays and Saturdays in Spital Square. At first it was a general market, but as the old Stocks market at Mansion House in the City became overcrowded, vegetable merchants moved out to Spital Square and began to dominate the market. It proved a good outlet for the market gardens of Inner Essex at West Ham, Barking and Plaistow, and was soon operating most days.

For nearly two hundred years Spitalfields market was a ramshackle collection of timber buildings. In 1876 the whole site was acquired by Robert Horner whose meteoric rise had rivalled the legend of Dick Whittington. Only twenty years earlier as a youth he had left his farm labourer's job in Essex to seek his fortune, becoming a market porter. Horner's persistence earned promotion to country buyer for one of the top salesmen and swiftly secured him a partnership. In 1876 he realized his dream, erected new buildings completed in 1893 at a cost of £80,000, and introduced a new system of tolls and rents. Horner was ruthlessly ambitious. He enforced the earlier charter of Charles II whereby no other fruit and vegetable market could operate in East London without paying tolls to Spitalfields, even including the new Stratford wholesale market opened five miles away by the Great Eastern Railway. Spitalfields' carts and wagons seriously obstructed Commercial Street, but proceedings taken against Horner were overruled due to the power of the charter. The tram company had to pay compensation to Horner before laying their tracks. He duly made his fortune.

However, in 1902 the City Corporation compulsorily acquired the market. After a thirteen-year legal battle which went to the Court of Appeal Horner was paid £284,500. The City embarked on a massive programme of expansion and improvement in 1922, widening Lamb Street, Brushfield Street and Steward Street to provide alternative access to Commercial Street and extending the buildings. Two million pounds was invested in modernization, including the new flower market built in 1935.

In 1928 the London Fruit Exchange moved from its old premises in Pudding Lane to new buildings on the south side of Brushfield Street, as an important complement to the market.

For the 1980s Spitalfields is remarkably healthy, with throughput steady or even increasing. There are 150 wholesalers within the market renting 226

Commercial Street 1908. Horse-drawn trams clatter past the gabled market buildings (G.L.C.)

stands. All available space is taken and any vacancy is quickly snapped up, such is the demand. The scale of operation and the bulkiness of the goods handled is colossal. Approximately 300,000 packages or boxes of fruit and vegetables are sold each day – in the order of 1,500 tons. Trading hours are limited to between 4.30 a.m. and 2.30 p.m. but lorries are arriving and unloading at all times, a trickle in the afternoons and a peak in the late evening. Each tenant employs his own salesmen, clerks and porters. There are no independent pitchers or bummarees. The 200 porters are licensed by the market superintendent on recommendation from the tenants and union, but otherwise there is little interference. The old-fashioned toll system was commuted in Horner's day and now

tenants only pay a rent and service charge. Only casual traders pay tolls.

Apart from telephone deals the market is not a sample market, and stock is displayed on the stands or stored in the huge basements. Forklift trucks and electric floats are used universally. The market constables control the traffic and little else. Theft is something of a problem, simply because of the sheer size of the place and the open type of operation. Some firms employ their own nightwatchmen.

Everything comes and goes by lorry, whether grown at home or abroad. Giant juggernauts arrive from Spain, France, Greece, Italy, Romania and Turkey. A lot of American, African and Australasian fruit is shipped to Rotterdam and then brought by container lorry – Fyffes and Geest

bananas for example. The lorry parks are already groaning under the strain. Although tenants have their regular senders Spitalfields is not a growers' market, unlike Borough or Covent Garden where growers' stands are specifically allocated.

Buyers come from all over London and the Home Counties, biased towards the north and east – greengrocers, hoteliers, caterers, buyers for supermarkets and multiple chains. Some of the larger buyers, like Marks and Spencer, deal through the Fruit Exchange. This trade is only in paper, not even using samples. Auctioning stopped in 1973, as part of the trend towards private treaty begun by the South African Citrus Board. The auction rooms were converted into squash courts and the warehouses into offices for shippers, insurance brokers and accountants.

The flower market on the north side of Lamb Street is Spitalfields' one small-scale enterprise. It has never competed in size with Covent Garden, and in 1978 the annex was demolished and the flower market consolidated into half of its original space. Nevertheless there is something attractive about the flower market that the fruit and vegetables lack. It was so constructed that the blooms would not be withered by direct sunlight, and in early spring the stands are ablaze with daffodils from the Scilly Isles, the air thick with the heavy scent of freesias.

Today about 1,700 people work in the fruit and vegetable business at Spitalfields, 1,000 in the market and 700 in the Exchange, where numbers have actually increased. The prospective 32 acres on Hackney Marshes will allow growth, even amalgamation with Stratford to form a unified East London market. The potential of old Spitalfields for lucrative redevelopment has spurred the financiers to provide a new £34 million market, free to the Corporation in return for the site. Everyone seems enthusiastic about Hackney Wick – well served by road and rail. Parliament has repealed Charles's Charter; we await 1991.

The existing buildings operate for the last lingering seasons. Architecturally they are nothing wonderful, though Horner's pleasantly gabled

façade to Commercial Street survives. Spitalfields has its old customs: several local pubs like the Gun in Brushfield Street open at 6 a.m., and in the middle of the main market is a jellied eel stall, a long-established tradition.

Outside market hours the wide roads and shutters make it rather bleak. A few old men with shopping bags sift through squashed cabbage leaves and grapefruits for edible remnants, or grapple with abandoned broken pallets for firewood. The austere west front and tower of Hawksmoor's Christchurch dominate the view along Brushfield Street. On a windy evening with dusk fallen it is easy to remember that these empty streets were the haunt of Jack the Ripper. Some think he even worked in the market. His ghost lives on in the dark alleys and shadowy doorways, chilling the spine. His anonymity ensures his place in history.

Stock Exchange, EC2

Merchandise: Stocks and shares.

Opening times: 9.30 a.m. to 3.30 p.m. Monday to Friday, on the trading floor. Public viewing gallery open during trading hours.

Location: North side of Threadneedle Street.

Nearest tube: Bank (Northern, Central).

Buses: Nos. 6, 8, 9, 11, 15, 21, 22, 25, 43, 76, 133, 149, 501 (Bank).

The Stock Exchange, like the Bank of England, is one of the most important institutions in the City, the financial hub of the economy. It is a market for money, dealing in stocks and shares, whose transactions affect directly or indirectly the livelihood of most British subjects. The Stock Exchange is a place which everyone has heard of but few really know. In *Pickwick Papers* the two Wellers 'proceeded from the Bank to the gate of the Stock Exchange, to which Wilkins Flasher Esq., after a short absence, returned with a cheque on Smith, Payne and Smith for £530, that being the sum of money to which Mr Weller, at the market price of the day, was entitled in consideration of the balance of the second Mrs Weller's funded savings'. That air of mystery and professional intrigue continues.

Stocks and shares were introduced early in the seventeenth century as a way of raising ready cash from the public for the Government and private companies. Anyone buying stocks and shares acquired a share in the company and, as a shareholder, benefited from profits made. They rapidly attracted investors and financiers and a regular market soon formed, at first meeting in the courtyard of the Royal Exchange. When a new beverage – coffee – became fashionable in the 1650s, the dealers moved to the new City coffee houses such as

Jonathans in Exchange Alley. Similarly shipping merchants patronized Edward Lloyd's coffee house in Lombard Street, birthplace of Lloyd's insurance.

Stocks and shares are a risk; in an age when gambling was rife they were irresistible. Dealers clamoured to share in the huge profits accruing from expanding overseas trade. The craze culminated in the hysteria of the South Sea Bubble, the famous crash of 1720, when the South Sea Trading Company accepted responsibility for the entire national debt of £51 million. The bubble burst, bankrupting thousands of investors, the biggest disaster in British financial history. The Chancellor of the Exchequer, Secretary of State and Postmaster General were held responsible and the disgraced Tories resigned, replaced by Walpole and the Whigs. 'The bubblers were bubbled.'

Thereafter dealing was more cautious and new regulations were established in a determined effort to recover face. Dr Johnson was not impressed; his dictionary defines the stock-jobber as 'a low wretch who gets money by buying and selling shares in the funds'. In 1773 the brokers rented their own building in Threadneedle Street and called it the Stock Exchange. Larger buildings were erected in 1853, designed by Thomas Allason. The veined marble pillars beneath the central dome earned it the nickname 'Gorgonzola Hall'. That, sadly, was replaced in 1973 by a huge concrete tower which is the Stock Exchange today.

Entry to the trading floor is restricted to members of the Stock Exchange. The public therefore cannot

Familiar view of the floor of the modern Stock Exchange

166

'Gorgonzola Hall' in 1957. The old Stock Exchange was demolished in 1973 (Guildhall Library)

buy stocks and shares direct but must employ stockbrokers to deal for them, although they can watch the transactions from the viewing gallery. On the floor of the Stock Exchange are sixteen hexagonal kiosks, each with a bench around the outside. These are the pitches of the 'jobbers', the wholesalers or principals who buy and sell stocks and shares on behalf of the companies or institutions who issue them. The pitches specialize in different commodities – gilts, industrial, foreign and mines. The British Government, unlike any other, manages its national debt on the floor of the Stock Exchange. These are the gilt-edged stocks, where money is raised for Government spending which cannot be met from taxation or loans from the Bank of England.

The jobbers sit or stand by their pitch (an improvement on Gorgonzola Hall where there were no seats) while the brokers circulate gathering and comparing prices. Jobbers quote two prices, one for buying, one for selling, all done by word of mouth. Most securities have at least two jobbers in competition; brokers buy at the best price for the time, taking $1\frac{1}{2}$ per cent commission on the deal. The two weeks' grace for accounting encourages speculation. The 'bull' buys shares whose value may rise, the 'bear' sells those which might fall. Deals are made verbally and written into notebooks, 'My word is my bond' in practice and motto.

The besuited people on the floor are distinguished by different coloured badges. Blue identifies juniors and unauthorized clerks. 'Blue buttons' are employed by jobbers and brokers to run messages and inquire prices but are not allowed to deal. Yellow badges denote authorized clerks who can deal on behalf of their firm. White badges signify fully fledged brokers who must first pass the onerous Stock Exchange examinations in taxation, investment, exchange practice and company reporting. Once all members had to wear top hats; now only the gilt-edged jobbers and older members carry on the tradition.

The attendants are still called waiters. Gate-crashers traditionally regretted their temerity, for they were greeted by rough hands and the cry of 'Fourteen hundred!', dating from the time when there were exactly 1,399 members of the London Stock Exchange. Women were admitted in 1973 into the chauvinist bastion, but represent a minute fraction of the 4,500 members today.

Brokers and jobbers are now equipped with numerous modern communication aids, tele-printers, video scanners, direct telephones to money markets all over the globe and two-way radios and bleepers linking the trading floor with the brokers' offices. Clocks mounted high on the wall tell the precise time in San Francisco, Toronto, New York, Zurich, Johannesburg, Tokyo, Hong Kong and Melbourne. The jet board splashes news in vivid green letters with a warning bell announcing major events. In pre-telegraph days the Rothschilds pioneered the use of carrier pigeons to bring continental news. Special reporters were sent to cover foreign campaigns.

Prices of stocks vary with supply and demand. The Financial Times Share Index Board, based on the thirty-six top industrial shares, shows the trend of the market. The Stock Exchange is a key to the economic well-being of the country, but is also famous for its flutters and jitters, reflecting all manner of political trivia. Sometimes the floor is remarkably quiet with jobbers and brokers milling around idly; in full panic the floor seethes with activity – blue-buttons rushing errands between kiosks, dealers shouting above the din.

The market is run by the Council of the Stock Exchange. Members pay an annual fee and elect the ruling committee who vet any company wishing to issue shares and dictate the controls for dealing. Above the trading floor, rising high over the City, are the brokers' offices where computers sort out the day's dealing, analysts sift figures and company reports, and telephone trading continues long after the floor has closed. The visitors' viewing gallery (open 9.45 a.m. to 3.15 p.m.) provides a marvellous panorama of the trading floor of the world's largest stock market. Each day 25,000 deals worth £600 million are done in up to 8,000 different securities, altogether worth £300,000 million. That's a lot of money, and just some of it is yours and mine.

Stratford, E15

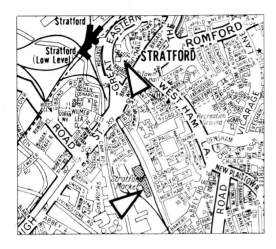

Merchandise: Wholesale fruit and vegetables.

Opening times: 6 a.m. to midday Monday; 4.30 a.m. to midday Tuesday to Saturday.

Location: South end of Burford Road, beside the railway.

Nearest tube: Stratford (Central).

Buses: Nos. 8A, 10, 25, 86, 108, 225, N76, N98.

Stratford market was built in 1879 by the Great Eastern Railway Company as a railhead for East Anglian produce and as a convenient centre for supplying East London. The sprawling suburbs of Ilford, Romford, Woodford and Leyton had smothered the once idyllic Essex pastures on the east bank of the River Lea. Stratford, the Saxon ford across the Lea, became an important railway junction and a sensible location for a wholesale market.

The market was constructed as two lines of warehouses, each 220 yards long, separated by a forty-foot-wide roadway. Railway tracks came right up to the back of each warehouse enabling fruit and vegetables to be unloaded straight into the stalls. The central roadway for the buyers' horse-drawn carts was roofed over giving a covered area of three and a half acres. Two hundred railway trucks could be unloaded simultaneously, and waiting or empty wagons occupied a further three acres of sidings.

At the outset the Railway Company had to fight a legal battle with the owner of Spitalfields market who claimed that the rights granted under royal charter were being infringed. Stratford won its case and in its heyday handled vast amounts of produce. Special trains thundered through the night to reach the market; the famous Whitemoor Vegetable Express arrived at Stratford at 4.15 a.m. Supplies came from the Continent via the Harwich–Zeebrugge ferry. Stratford was among the first markets to import bananas – in 1890 they were considered strange and costly, but within twenty years they had become commonplace and cheap, largely due to the endeavours of Fyffes. Peculiar railway vans, steam-heated in winter, cooled in summer, carried the Jamaican banana bunches

CHAS. F. FRENCH,
ROOT & VEGETABLE SALESMAN & COMMISSION AGENT
HAY, STRAW, CHAFF, CORN AND FORAGE CONTRACTOR,
6, STRATFORD MARKET & DUNMOW ROAD STEAM CHAFF CUTTING FORAGE STORE

Liberal Contracts made with large Buyers, Schools, Public Institutions, &c. Prices on application.

All orders and Communications to be addressed to 6, Stratford Market, to which prompt attention will be

Above: Victorian optimism (Newham Library)
Below: Recession, 100 years on

from Liverpool's docks. In addition to fruit and vegetables Stratford sold general farm produce – hay, straw, chaff, corn and forage – and many of the original tenants were growers with their own farms.

Today the market is a shabby rundown affair, dealing mainly in ordinary vegetables and no longer rivalling the central wholesale markets. British Rail still owns it, although it tried selling to the tenants in 1968. Redevelopment proposals in 1955 and 1972, when there was talk of Spitalfields moving out, were abandoned because of poor road access. Now B.R. has no money to improve the old slatted timber buildings, reminiscent of rural station architecture. Nothing arrives by rail; Beeching castrated it and most of the tracks have been taken up or overgrown. B.R. collects tolls on lorries (rail-borne produce was exempted) and rents from the forty tenants. Most are commission sellers, and some like Wilderspin (potatoes) and Marsh (mushrooms) also operate from Covent Garden, Borough or Spitalfields.

Trading starts at 4.30 a.m., later on Monday, and is finished by midday. A few traders occupy the peeling 1930s sheds in Burford Road, while Channelsea Road with Donovan Bros. Paper Bag Makers and the Market Canteen looks equally forlorn. The traders' association have negotiated in vain for improvements. Meanwhile the market declines. On the east side of Burford Road the impressive but empty warehouse, four storeys of blue and red engineering bricks, is being converted into workshops. These may bring new life to the Burford Arms, which opens for the market between 7 and 10 each morning.

Stratford Broadway is an ancient highway, used in the mid nineteenth century as a cattle market and fairground. Costermongers lined the High Street and Angel Lane gutters and though the local board tried to move them they always returned. Nearly a century later the street market was allocated space in a new covered shopping mall, the Stratford Centre. In the north wing of the precinct twenty-nine brightly lit stalls offer a good selection of fresh fruit and veg., wet and shellfish, and two excellent stands sell wool and haberdashery, a boon

for local knitters. The Stratford Centre is as spry and sprightly as the wholesale market is seedy and scruffy – two contrasting facets to the capricious market story.

Appendix: The Suburbs

Any compilation inevitably has its limitations. This book has concentrated on the markets of inner London and consciously omitted detailed descriptions of the numerous and excellent markets in the suburbs. One has to stop somewhere.

As a humble appeasement, and perhaps as a foretaste of a much-needed volume covering the provinces, the following are some of the best suburban markets.

Bromley, Station Road, in car park: Thursday.

Croydon, Surrey Street: Monday to Saturday – a small busy fruit and vegetable market.

Dartford, Market Place: Monday to Saturday, beside the Arndale Centre.

Edmonton, Market Square: Tuesday to Saturday.

Enfield, Market Place: Thursday and Saturday, in the old market square.

Epping, High Street: Monday and Friday.

Epsom: Saturday, beside the clock tower.

Erith, Pier Road: Wednesday and Saturday.

Feltham, High Street, in car park behind old theatre: Thursday and Saturday.

Finchley, Ballards Lane: Friday and Saturday.

Kingston-upon-Thames, Apple Market: Monday to Saturday – a famous market with an ancient charter. Fairfield Market: Monday only.

Romford, Market Place: Wednesday, Friday and Saturday – once a cattle market, now 200 general stalls.

Southall: 8 a.m. to dusk, on the south side of the High Street, next to the park. Wednesday – horse auction (also goats) frequented by gipsies, country folk and rag-and-bone men. Thursday – second-hand market. Saturday – general market.

St Albans, High Street: Wednesday and Saturday.

Sutton, West Street: Tuesday and Saturday.

Tooting Broadway: Monday to Saturday.

Uxbridge, Market Square: Friday and Saturday.

Waltham Abbey: Tuesday and Saturday – a picturesque setting off Abbey View.

Watford: Tuesday, Friday and Saturday, in an enclosed market off the High Street.

Wealdstone, Station Road: Friday and Saturday, in the football ground car park.

Wembley: Sunday market in stadium car park.

Western International, Heston: Modern wholesale fruit and vegetable market beside the M4, Junction 3. Also general market on Sunday.

Bibliography

Aldous, A., *The Illustrated London News Book of London's Villages* (Secker & Warburg, 1980).

Bebbington, G., *London Street Names* (Batsford, 1972).

Benedetta, M., *Street Markets of London* (John Miles, 1936).

Campbell, S., *Guide to Good Food Shops* (Macmillan, 1979).

Clout, H. (ed.), *Changing London* (University Tutorial Press, 1978).

Cooper, J., *London's Antique Street Markets* (Thames & Hudson, 1974).

Curtis, R., *East End Passport* (Macdonald, 1969).

Dodd, C., *Food in London* (1858).

Fisherman, W. J., *The Streets of East London* (Gerald Duckworth, 1979).

Forshaw, A., and Bergström, T., *Smithfield Past and Present* (Heinemann, 1980).

Gibson-Jarvie, R., *The City of London: A Financial and Commercial History* (Woodhead-Faulkner, 1979).

Harris, C., *Islington* (Hamish Hamilton, 1974).

Hibbert, C., *London: The Biography of a City* (Penguin, 1980).

Howgego, J. L., *London in the Twenties and Thirties* (Batsford, 1978).

Howgego, J. L., *Victorian and Edwardian City of London* (Batsford, 1977).

Jenkins, V., *Where I Was Young* (Granada, 1976).

Kent, W., *An Encyclopaedia of London* (Dent, 1970).

London County Council Public Control Department, 'Report of existing markets and market rights' (1896).

London Transport Executive, *The London of Charles Dickens* (Midas Books, 1979).

Mackenzie, G., *Marylebone* (Macmillan, 1972).

Maugham, C., *Markets in London* (Pitman, 1931).

Mayhew, H., *London Labour and the London Poor* (1851).

Metcalf, P., *Victorian London* (Cassell, 1972).

Passingham, W. J., *London's Markets* (Samson Low, 1934).

Robertson, A. B., 'The Open Market in the City of London' (*East London Papers*, Vol. I, 1958).

Robertson, D. W., *Chaucer's London* (Wiley & Sons, 1968).

Rudé, G., *Hanoverian London 1714–1808* (Secker & Warburg, 1971).

Seaman, L. C. B., *Life in Victorian London* (Batsford, 1973).

Sheppard, F., *London 1808–1870: the Infernal Wen* (Secker & Warburg, 1971).

Sinclair, R., *East London* (Robert Hale, 1950).

Stow, J., *The Survey of London* (1598).

Trevelyan, G. M., *English Social History* (Longmans, 1942).

Farringdon Road

Geographical Index

(Italics have been used for markets and fairs no longer operating.)

Geographical Index

Commodity Index

The following retail markets are particularly good for the commodities listed below

Antiques and jewellery
Bermondsey SE1, 106
Camden Lock NW1, 110
Camden Passage N1, 112
Church Street NW8 & W2, 54
Greenwich SE10, 121
Jubilee Market WC2, 66
London Silver Vaults WC2, 126
Portobello Road W10 & W11, 131

Books
Bell Street NW1, 105
Camden Passage N1, 112
Earlham Street WC2, 66
Exmouth Market EC1, 118
Farringdon Road EC1, 119
Greenwich SE10, 121
Piccadilly W1, 104
Russell Square WC1, 136
South Bank SE1, 120
Swiss Cottage NW3, 93

Bric-à-brac and junk
Bell Street NW1, 105
Brick Lane E1 & E2, 42
Camden Lock NW1, 110
Church Street NW8 & W2, 54
Douglas Way SE8, 57
Hackney Stadium E15, 123
Portobello Road W10 & W11, 131
Swiss Cottage NW3, 92
Westmoreland Road SE17, 137

Clothes, new
Brick Lane E1 & E2, 42
Brixton SW9, 44
Camden Lock NW1, 110
Chalton Street NW1, 114
Chapel Market N1, 48
Chrisp Street E14, 52
East Street SE17, 58
Jubilee Market WC2, 66
Kilburn Square NW6, 124
Leather Lane EC1, 73
Lower Marsh SE1, 77
Nags Head N7, 127
Petticoat Lane E1, 128
Queen's Crescent NW5, 82

Rathbone Street E16, 84
Roman Road E3, 134
Shepherd's Bush W12, 86
Walthamstow High Street E17, 94
Whitecross Street EC1, 100

Clothes, second-hand
Bell Street NW1, 105
Brick Lane E1 & E2, 42
Camden Lock NW1, 110
Douglas Way SE8, 57
Hackney Stadium E15, 123
Hoxton Street N1, 63
Nags Head N7, 127
Petticoat Lane E1, 128
Portobello Road W10 & W11, 131
Roman Road E3, 134
Swiss Cottage NW3, 92

Crafts
Bayswater Road W2, 104
Camden Lock NW1, 110
Gabriel's Wharf SE1, 120
Greenwich SE10, 121
Hampstead Community Market NW3, 61
Jubilee Market WC2, 66
Lewisham High Street SE13, 75
Piccadilly W1, 104
Swiss Cottage NW3, 92

Fish and seafood
Beresford Square SE18, 37
Bethnal Green Road E2, 41
Brixton SW9, 44
Broadway Market E8, 46
Catford Broadway SE6, 47
Chapel Market N1, 48
Exmouth Market EC1, 118
Hammersmith W6, 60
Leadenhall EC3, 71
Nags Head N7, 127
Queen's Market E13, 83
Southwark Park Road SE16, 89
Tachbrook Street SW1, 93
Walthamstow High Street E17, 94

Fruit and vegetables
Beresford Square SE18, 37
Berwick Street W1, 38
Brixton SW9, 44
Chapel Market N1, 48

Commodity Index